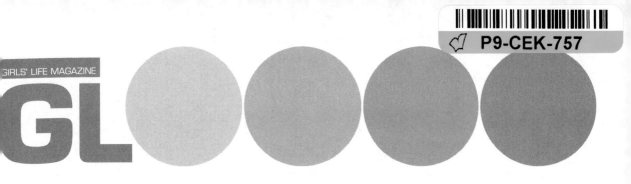

GIRLS' LIFE MAGAZINE

GL

The Girls' Life
must-Have guide
to making
and keeping FrienDs

Edited by Karen Bokram and Jodi Lynn Bryson

Scholastic Inc.
New York • Toronto • London • Auckland • Sydney
Mexico City • New Delhi • Hong Kong • Buenos Aires

ISBN: 0-439-44975-8

Design: Mark Neston
Illustrations: Lisa Parett

12 11 10 9 8 7 6 5 4   3 4 5 6 7 8/0

Printed in the U.S.A.

First Scholastic printing, January 2003

contents

Question…who are the three most important people in your life right now? Your mom? Dad? Big sister? Chances are, more than a few of you answered with names of your friends. As much as you love your 'rents and your sibs, this is the time in your life when your friends take front row seats. Bet it's hard to imagine where you'd be, or who you'd be, without your pack of pals or your one super-special, best friend forever (BFF).

From our very first years, our friends play a crucial role in our lives. While almost everyone makes their first friends thanks to Mom (the Pamper pals), most of us are now very much on our own when it comes to making and keeping friends.

And the cool thing is that you can have all kinds of friends! It's great to have a BFF—someone you find beyond special. And how much fun is it to have a great group of gals to hang out with? And don't forget about casual school buds—the ones who are always up for sharing a laugh in the halls. And how about summer buds—the ones you only see for a few weeks each year, but who you're still super-close with? Awesome!

But as fabulous as friends can be, they can be equally stressful. It takes time and confidence to become better friends with the girl in math class you like, but only chat with before and after class. And what if you're worried about a friend blabbing your deepest secret? Or what if you and your BFF suddenly can't agree on a thing? Sooner or later, you might just find yourself neck-deep in a full-blown bud-battle that threatens a friendship. Ah! These bugaboos linger and threaten the walls of even the strongest, most solid bud bonds.

Ever wish someone would tell you how to navigate through the tricky land of friendship? Well wish no more!

Enter your very own foolproof, girls-only, must-have guide to making and keeping friends! GL has the answers! We gathered, snooped, and spied until we got the skinny on it all. What you are holding in your hands is a GL-made map for navigating around the twists and turns, and ups and downs, of the rough and tumble roads you'll encounter along your friendship journey.

Your friendship trip is probably already well on its way, but there's a reason you'll need maps and compasses—sometimes travel plans change. In this book, you'll learn that it's great to stay on the same, safe road you've always traveled (no sense in getting lost if you already like where you are). But you'll learn that it's also OK to switch directions and take some new, unfamiliar roads, too.

Some quick words of advice? *Don't forget to buckle your seatbelt!* It might be a bumpy ride. *Watch for dead ends!* If the road doesn't look like it goes anywhere, it probably doesn't. *Avoid reckless drivers and litter bugs!* They're rude and sure to get you in trouble—take an alternate route. *Be wary of one-way streets!* They can be lonely. *Obey traffic signals!* If you see a red light, stop. If it's yellow, slow down and look around. And if the light turns green, go for it!

Oh, and if you're confused, lost, or think you're in a dangerous neighborhood, for goodness sake—stop and browse through this book for directions. That's what we're here for. *Bon Voyage!*

Karen

Karen Bokram,
Editor-in-Chief, GL

Factoring in new Friends

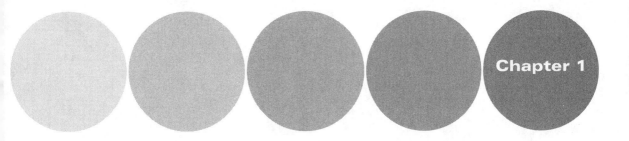

Chapter 1

make new Friends anywhere, anytime!

Ally is 12 and has lived in seven states, attended nine schools, and has ten best friends. Ally's dad is in the Army so her family moves a bunch. As a result, Ally has perfected the art of making friends.

Jumpstart a Friendship

As Ally's learned, there are a lot of places to scope out potential new buds and tons of ways to jumpstart a friendship. Making friends doesn't mean doing anything nuts, like daringly announcing to a group of girls at the food court that you want to join their clique. Becoming friends with someone is, as Ally knows, an art. And you, friendly girl, are about to become a BFF artist! If you truly want to make new friends, use these new-friend-making tactics anywhere, anytime.

In Class

Try to think of class as more than just blackboards and erasers. It's your chance to get a good glimpse at what kind of friend a classmate might make. Who's giving everyone the low down on what happened on your favorite show last night? Who has the scoop on the tryouts for the school play? Who just made the track team? Which girl is the one who everyone rushes to for great advice? Who loves to sit and read the latest *Harry Potter* book or just chill out and daydream? By being tuned in to who likes what, some gals are bound to pique your interest as potential pals.

So how *do* you get to know girls whose interests interest you? One thing's for sure—not many people can resist a friendly invite. Let's say you're in fifth period math class and you realize there's a girl who's into gymnastics (like you are), but not so good at algebra (which you're a whiz at). Before class, walk up to her, smile, and say, "I was thinking about putting together a study group before the big algebra test on Friday. Are you interested?" If she's up for it, suggest she bring along some other girls. That way, you only have to approach one girl, and she'll do the rest.

Between practicing math problems, bring up how much you love your new gymnastics coach. Your new friend is bound to respond, and now you have *two* things in common—

school and a sport. Then maybe another girl will chime in about how her sister is the state champ on the balance beam. Suddenly, you're all off and talking! See how it works?

While chatting, don't forget to be a good listener, too, and ask the others what kind of stuff they're into. If you hit it off with someone, exchange phone numbers or e-mail addresses. Easy as 1-2-3!

What Won't Work

Whatever you do, don't approach your target-friend just as your teacher is trying to get everyone settled and say, "I'm really into gymnastics, and you need help in math. Will you be my friend?" That's too overwhelming for anyone! Casual and friendly wins them over every time.

On a Team

You don't exactly emulate Mia Hamm? You've got two left feet? Even if you don't fancy yourself an athlete, joining a team or playing intra-mural can *teach* you the sport. Do you run fast? Go for track. Are you great at video games? Try out for a sport requiring good hand/eye coordination, like tennis or basketball. The girls you play with could become your favorite people—and you theirs.

No group is more bonded than team-mates. And that's because teams bring together all the elements of being friends—trust, communication, and commitment. Plus, being part of a team is fun, exciting, and challenging. The great part is that you and your teammates share a common goal—wanting to crush your rivals! Nothing wrong with a little healthy competi-tion, and you automatically have something in common with the other players. Plus you get lots of hang time during practices, work-outs, meet-ings, and bus rides to games and tournaments. Nothing builds cama-raderie quite like sharing in the thrill of victory and the agony of defeat. It's the stuff *close* friends are made of!

What won't Work

Don't offer to help your hopeful new friend with her batting style because you think she swings like a 3-year-old trying to hold a broom!

In a Club

Are you an environmental enthusiast, an animal activist, an Oscar-worthy actress, or a trivia whiz? Well, what's stopping you? Get your name down on that sign-up sheet! School clubs are terrific for making friends—mostly because everyone *chooses* a club they're into, unlike your run-of-the-mill history class where not everyone shares the same affection for ancient Egypt. But just because you're in Spanish Club doesn't mean you'll only sit around and speak *en español*. You and your *amigas* have fund-raisers to plan, school events to organize, trips to beg the administration for, and much, *much* more!

And, hey, if you're antsy to uncover some fellow

HELP!

I switched schools this year and met three new friends. They're all popular and say I am, too. But they only like to confide in each other. It's not like they ignore me, but I just feel left out a lot. What should I do?

It's hard to be the new girl in a group of old friends. Hang in there, and just take things a little more slowly. Once they get to know you better, hopefully they'll feel more comfy confiding in you and letting you in on their secrets and such. Make sure these girls are true friends and that you're not just being influenced by their "popularity." If they *are* true-blue pals, you should tell them how you feel. Let them know how much you enjoy their company, but that you feel left out sometimes and wish they would level with you. Know that it takes time to earn trust, but down the line they ought to make the effort to be more inclusive of you. If they still leave you out of their gabfests, consider getting to know some girls who seem like they'd be into a loyal new friend.

insect aficionados, why not start your own Insect Lovers club? Not only will new friends come to *you*, but is there anything cooler than a president/vice-president BFF duo? Your new web of pals will be talking dung beetles until you practically tear up from exoskeleton-insect joy!

As a Tutor

Helping a pal score an A is a genius way to strut your friendly stuff. If you're tutor material, you'll get the inside scoop on what classmates are like one-on-one. Heck, the girl who annoyingly cracks her gum might turn out to be pretty cool. If math is a walk in the park for you, hold study sessions. Maybe some of your clueless math tutees are word whizzes and you could get a little help with your English essays. Barter your tutoring skills: "Hey, seems like English is a cinch for you. But I'm not doing so well. I'd be more than happy to walk you through algebra if you'll help me

string together a complete sentence." You might just land yourself a new friend!

On Your Block

When you were six, making friends was as easy as walking up to some kid and saying, "Wanna play hop-scotch?" Worked didn't it? So why give up on a good thing? What's so tough about asking the girl who lives three houses down from you if she wants to volunteer with you for the neighborhood cleanup? Approaching a neighbor is easy because she probably already knows you as the girl in the yellow house. Next time she's out in her yard, wander down the street. A simple, "Hey, what's up?

I live in the yellow house and I've always meant to stop by and say hi," is a great way to start.

At the Library

The library gets a bad rep. But those book havens don't have to be boring, stuffy, dusty, or dull. The library can actually be a pretty cool place to hang out—and meet friends (especially during the sweltering summer months!). Tons of people hit it up for free online access. Check out local libraries for teen book clubs and talk about your favorite reads with people who are book lovers like you. Keep an eye out for bulletin board announcements of craft shows, teen book fairs, tutoring programs, and clubs. When the girl next to you says, "What did you think of the last *Harry Potter*?" smile and tell her why you loved it (or didn't love it). From there, you just might become fast friends.

At a Theme Park

Skate parks, water parks, and mini-golf parks rule. Everyone's having fun and there are so many people to hook up with. Lots of times, there are teams needing one more player or a friendly group looking for one more person to play a game, so going alone to a park

I am going to a new camp this summer for soccer. I don't know anyone else who's going.

Nobody likes being the new girl. It's intimidating, no matter how confident you are. Finding something to chat about is often the hardest step, but you already have soccer in common. And the best part about sports camp? It's so activity-intensive that you're never just standing around thinking of stuff to say—you're running, doing drills, scrimmaging and playing a game you love. Says Jennifer: "A couple summers ago, I went to lacrosse camp. I didn't know anyone, and I was nervous. The first day, I got up the guts to ask a group of girls playing catch if I could join in. We had a great time and ended up getting to know each other really well. We're all still friends!" Remind yourself that you're not the only new girl—other girls are in the same sitch. Be friendly, smile and take the initiative. If the coach instructs you to partner up, don't stare at your cleats—turn to the girl next to you and introduce yourself.

YOUR HELP!

Whenever my new BFF comes over to my house, she totally ignores me and hangs out with my older brother. I feel like my friend uses me to get to my brother. She thinks he's "cute."

When this happened to me, I made an effort to get out and have a great time with my BFF. Instead of just hanging around the house, we went to the mall and stuff. If we were busy, she wasn't as concerned with my brother.

—*Lisa, 11*

Be honest, and explain how you feel. Good friends need to communicate. If she doesn't agree with you, kick him out of the house when she comes over. If he's not around, she can't pay attention to him!

—*Amanda, 12*

I would talk with my friend and tell her I feel left out. If she doesn't like what I'm saying, then she really isn't my friend.

—*Sarah, 11*

I would confront my BFF and tell her how I feel. If it turned out she was using me, then she probably wasn't a friend in the first place.

—*Alanna, 10*

It can be hard to tell when a friend is over if she's there to see you or your hottie brother. Talk to her; maybe she doesn't realize how you feel. For one-on-one time, go to her house. And, remember, she *is* allowed to think a guy is cute!

—*Laura, 12*

isn't a bad idea *at all*. Grab your skates, your bathing suit, or your golf glove, and get over there. Challenge someone to a race down the steepest slide. See if that girl will show you how to pull off her stellar half-pipe trick. Ask if anyone's up for some one-on-one mini-golf. Parks are for playing, so have fun!

What won't work

Don't complain about the long waits in line, the heat, the quality of the half-pipe, or the water. No one likes a complainer.

summer sisters

Stuck at summer camp and none of your friends from home came along? Make a solo situation into a great time with the quick fix of a new friend.

"Even though I only have a few weeks with my friends from camp, those are some of the best weeks of my year—and some of the best friends I have," says Madison, 11, a three-year camp veteran. While it might seem easier just to hide under the nearest swim dock, instead of introducing yourself to complete strangers—just do it! Everyone else is there to make friends, too. Here are some hints for getting the friend-making ball rolling.

Say "hi."

"Walk over to the person and say, 'Hi, my name is Ali, what's yours?' Sounds beyond simple but it works."
—Allison, 10

Don't limit yourself.

"You could miss out on a great friend if you dismiss a girl just because she doesn't seem like *your* type of person. Find out if you have common interests. Be open and honest, and that'll let other girls know they can be open and honest with you, too."
—Lucy, 11

Find an icebreaker.

"I was waiting for a hot dog with another girl, and the guy making them was slow. I turned to the girl and said, 'Looks like we're not the only ones on vacation here!' She laughed, and I introduced myself."
—Tara, 11

Get involved.

"Focus on having a great time. Be yourself, but don't be the one who never wants to do what the group is doing. Take part in activities and remember to compromise."
—Emily, 10

Be friendly, and put the other person first.

"You can make a person feel really good by making her the subject of your sentence. Try my trick. Instead of saying something like, 'I love your sweater!', say, 'You look great in that sweater.' That puts the focus on your new friend."

—Sarah, 11

Be brave.

Jenna reminds herself that if someone isn't friendly back, it probably has nothing to do with her and everything to do with the unfriendly person. "I say in my head, 'I don't sound like a dork; I sound friendly.' After all, what would I think if someone tried to be nice to me? I'd think she was pretty cool!"

—Jenna, 9

Friend...or Foe?

A potentially great friend is often the person you least expect. Even a sworn enemy could someday be your best bud. Don't scoff, because an enemy-turned-BFF can happen—and happily does a lot of times. Think about someone you butt heads with a lot. Now keep that "enemy" in mind while you read each of these anti-friend reasons to figure out if friction is ruining what could be a fine friendship.

She gossips about you.

Could it be that this person's not actually gossiping, but somehow getting blamed for spreading rumors about you? Some girls are easy targets for girls who want to blame others for bad words. Maya, 13, was enemies with Alisha because Maya's best friend, Meghan, said Alisha was the gossiping source of some nasty talk. Alisha, who hates confrontation, took

Emily suddenly realized how cool Sarah was. Now all three girls are best friends.

She's part of a rival team, club, or clique.

Just because one girl is a cheerleader and another is in band, doesn't mean that the two are incompatible! Or, if some girl scored the winning basket against you in a game, remember that it's just a game. And then get over it! If a girl is friends with a different group of friends than your group? Big deal! It's not "your crew versus her crew," so why not invite her and her friends on a weekend outing with you and your friends?

When Debbie met Gabrielle, Debbie was a shy girl who hung out with two equally shy friends, and Gabrielle was an outgoing athlete who hung out with a high-profile clique. Debbie always thought Gabrielle was a snob, and Gabrielle always thought Debbie was a nerd. When they got assigned to work on a report together, they spent three weeks getting to know each other, and discovered that they made each other laugh…a lot. Now Debbie and her buds hang out on weekends with Gabrielle and her friends, and wonder why they all didn't get together sooner!

the fall to avoid a fight. Months later, Maya learned the truth when she overheard Meghan dissing her. Maya then realized Alisha wasn't a mean trash talker, she was just unsure of how to handle the sticky situation. Once the air was cleared, the two became fast friends and left back-stabbing Meghan behind.

She's the girl who took your best friend away.

Like it or not, no friend is your property. Your best friend is allowed to be friends with whomever she pleases (you'll just want to be sure she continues to treat you nicely). If you find yourself fighting with another girl over a friend, you may need to understand what's really going on. When Emily had it out with Sarah, the new girl in her group, Sarah assured Emily she didn't want to *steal* Kim, she just wanted more friends, and

Quiz

What's Your Friend Potential?

Find out whether or not you're as ideal a friend as you hope to be!

A best friend is the girl who tells the cute new boy he can't sit next to her on the bus because she's saving the spot for you. A best friend is there for you to call when you're tossing and turning over a big problem. A best friend stands up to even the most popular girl if she's taunting you. We'd all like a best friend we can count on 100 percent of the time. But friendship is a two-way street—**you have to be a good friend to have a best friend**.

Are you ideal friend material? Take this quiz to find out.

1 **Your friend tells you she'll meet you at the mall at 3 p.m. At 4 p.m., she finally saunters in. You:**

   a: walk away quickly before she sees you. You don't want her to know you've waited so long for her to show up.

   b: walk over and ask, "Where were you?" When she apologies and explains that her mother needed her to watch her younger brother, you forgive her on the spot.

   c: still spend time shopping with her, but it's hard to have fun because you're still angry with her for disrespecting you.

2 **Your best friend secretly tells you she has a crush on the new boy in school. You:**

   a: explain to her nicely that he's not that cute and practically the whole school hates him already.

   b: tell someone who might tell the boy discreetly so that he and your friend can have a chance to talk.

   c: offer encouragement and promise never to tell a soul. Your lips are zipped.

3 **You and your best friend fight:**

a: probably once a month.

b: almost never.

c: when you disagree on something (not that you really consider that fighting).

4 **In the hall, you overhear a group of girls talking about your friend. You:**

a: go up to those girls and say, "She's really nice—not a back-stabber like *some* people."

b: keep walking. Girls gossip, and if you say something, it could turn into a big drama.

c: tell your friend the whole thing so she knows who her real friends are.

5 **You and your friend both try out for the track team. She makes it, but you don't. You:**

a: congratulate her— this is a big accomplishment!

b: secretly avoid her for a few days. You were supposed to do it together.

c: pretend to be happy for her, but really feel bummed for yourself.

6 **You are on the way to a swim meet when your friend calls and says she just had a fight with her mom and needs someone to talk to. You:**

a: tell her you're really sorry but you have to go.

b: talk to her for about 10 minutes on your mom's cell on the way to the meet, then tell her you'll call her the second you get back.

c: blow off the meet and talk to your friend for as long as she needs.

7 **You and your friend are disagreeing about what movie to see. You:**

a: let her choose. It's not that big a deal.

b: argue about it until she finally gives in.

c: make a deal to see what she wants to see this time, and what you want to see next time.

8 **You and your best friend will be "Best Friends Forever", right?**

a: Yes! You wouldn't be able to live without her.

b: Maybe. Who knows? Something could happen to squash the friendship.

c: Never say forever. You're sure you'll both find new friends eventually, but it's cool for now.

SCORING

Add up your points to find out what kind of friend you truly are.

1.	**a:** 1	**b:** 3	**c:** 2	5.	**a:** 3	**b:** 1	**c:** 2
2.	**a:** 2	**b:** 1	**c:** 3	6.	**a:** 1	**b:** 2	**c:** 3
3.	**a:** 1	**b:** 2	**c:** 3	7.	**a:** 2	**b:** 1	**c:** 3
4.	**a:** 3	**b:** 1	**c:** 2	8.	**a:** 3	**b:** 1	**c:** 2

19-24 points: **Friends for Life**

Anyone would be lucky to have a friend as giving and caring as you. You realize friends are precious, and you'll do whatever it takes to make sure a friendship runs smoothly. But there is a small problem: Could you actually be *too* good a friend? There's a fine line between being there no matter what and being taken advantage of. You're very giving, so for this to be an ideal friendship, your friend has to be giving, too. In a solid, worthwhile relationship, both friends put in effort and are willing to compromise. If she's as generous as you are, you are one lucky pair of BFFs.

13-18 points: **Fine Friends**

You seem to have found the perfect balance of give-and-take in a friendship. You can be a wonderful bud, but you don't give so much of yourself that you sacrifice your own needs. You do all you can, when you can. You give your bud priority, and you trust she'll do the same for you. Enjoy the good times (as you have been), and stay alert when a friend is having a tough time. Friends are really banking on you in times of need, and the payoff is worth its weight in gold.

8-12 points: Need Help Friend

Time to up that Friend IQ! First, assess your friendly style: Are you considerate of other people's feelings? Are you putting yourself out there? Do you listen to what others say? Decide to be the best kind of friend you can be, and go for it! Introduce yourself to other girls, be open, and spend less time being concerned with yourself. *You've got to give friendship to receive friendship*, so if you're finding yourself without good friends, it's time to start giving attention, time, and support to others. If you do, it will come back to you. That's a promise.

YOUR HELP!

I've made a new friend, but she's extremely clingy and possessive. I don't know how to deal with her. I want her as a friend, but I need some space. She's there like 24-7!

Speak with her privately and explain that you feel smothered. Then try to lie low for a couple weeks. If she really cares about you as a friend, she will hopefully try to take it down a couple notches.
—*Nicole, 10*

Tell her how you feel. If she's really your friend, she'll understand that you need time for yourself. If not, then she isn't worthy of your friendship anyway, and you shouldn't let her get to you.
—*Helen, 11*

I'd say, "Look, you're really great, but I need some space. I want to stay friends, but a little less time between us will be much better! And another thing, don't be so possessive. Please don't be offended, OK?"
—*Carissa, 12*

This happened to me. This girl was constantly in my face. I finally told her I needed alone time. She didn't understand at first. I had to explain I wanted to be her friend—just not every waking moment.
—*Ginny, 10*

The Ties That Bond

Chapter 2

The 10 sacred rules of friendship

You have many different kinds of friends. But whether it's your best friend or the chatty bud you only see in math class, how you treat *all* your friends matters.

Thou Shalt...

...keep secrets sacred

Friendship is built on trust, and trusting a friend with a secret is a sacred part of that trust. When a bud trusts you with private stuff, whether it's whispers of a new crush or info about a personal matter, don't tell a single soul. A true friend knows secrets are secret! Such unquestionable confidence is the beauty of true-blue friendship. If you've been bogged down by a secret you want to unload, you want a friend who will keep that secret, no ifs, ands, or buts. Without a doubt, you owe the same courtesy to your friends. But slip-ups

happen. If you've slipped and spilled or your bud has, you know how tricky things can get. Spilling secrets can seriously injure even the best of friendships. To avoid letting out the really important secrets, be clear about which tidbits are just tidbits... and which are sacred. Before sharing, remind your bud, "This is a BIG deal, and I'm only telling *you*. So whatever you do, keep this to yourself." Same goes for the next time your bud lets you in on something. Ask her if what she's telling you is private. If so, keep your lips zipped. If you have a history of blabbing, be honest, and, before she shares, say, "I'm flattered, but I can't promise I won't tell." Friends respect that. It's better to miss out on a couple of secrets than to spill even one. If you're a secret-keeper, your friends will know it and will hold you in the highest regard. Bottom line? Keep secrets secret!

...not hold grudges

Your bud totally bummed you out when she insisted on cooking up a boatload of mac 'n' cheese, turning your mom's spotless kitchen into a disaster area. After chowing down, she didn't even clean up! When Mom came home, she freaked out on *you*! Taking the blame for something that technically wasn't your fault might make any girl a bit mad. But a true friend doesn't hold it against her pal. A true friend gives her pal the benefit of the doubt—even if she's stuck scraping cheese off the kitchen ceiling! She won't yell, throw a fit, sell her pal out to her not-so-happy mom, or punish her with silence. Whether you're a little upset or steaming-mad, take a breath and count to

ten before you speak. When you're super-mad, you run the risk of saying stuff you'll regret. Once you've chilled, explain the problem calmly without going off—your pal might not even know she let you down. Tell her your mom flipped and to be more considerate next time she has a mac 'n' cheese attack. If she's a good friend, she'll apologize big-time. If she's a *great* friend, she'll take the heat the next time she sees your mom—or she'll call her on the spot to apologize! Either way, she should definitely extend you the same courtesy if you happen to wind up on her mad list.

...provide tissues and tubs of ice cream as needed

Remember the last time you were so upset you couldn't stop crying? Likely, a let-it-all-out bawl session made you feel a bit better. But chances are, you needed more to get back on top of the world. That's where friends come in. When you feel like crawling under your covers and hibernating for a month, the comfort and support of a good friend is second to none. If you've been there, you know that even the smallest gesture can work wonders for a sad soul. So, if your friend is suffering a serious crisis or even a minor mishap, be there with TLC and don't judge. A real friend understands that when her bud is upset, that's all that matters. She senses when her friend needs a confidante, and understands when she needs to be alone. Offer your shoulder to lean on, a handful of tissues to blot the tears and some mint chocolate chip to sweeten the sadness. Pen her a note reminding her how special she is. Call before bedtime to let her know you're thinking about her. Make a batch of her favorite peanut butter brownies and leave them on her porch. Whatever it takes, find a way to make her smile and convince her that everything will be all right...because it really will.

...listen, really *listen*

Sure, friends can *hear* each other, but good friends *listen*—and there's a difference. Listening takes practice. Really! Just being quiet or waiting your turn to speak isn't truly listening— even though it might seem like it. Look at your friend when she's talking, and concentrate on what she's saying. Whether she has a funny tale to tell or she's seeking your advice, she won't appreciate talking to your ponytail while you paint your toenails. Plus, that's just plain rude! If your friend tells you something, you can pretty much bet she's telling you for a reason. Instead of tuning out, stop what you're doing, look at her and absorb her words. Consider this: If the absolute most embarrassing thing ever just happened to you and you're dying to tell her, you'd probably want her to say more than, "Uh, wait, what happened?"

...be as dependable as the rising sun

Being friends means you can count on each other every day, not every other day. Friends aren't socks, so it's not too cool to change them daily. A real friend isn't going to hang with a particular group of gals one morning and then diss them for another group two days later. Ew! Fickle friends aren't real friends. Friends are there for each other for fun stuff like birthdays and lazy Sunday afternoons. And friends don't disappear when stuff's not so fun, like when one of you needs mega help cramming for a math exam. And, *true* friends never ditch each other for a "better offer"! Presto change-o in the bud department makes you a fair-weather friend— you're around when things are good, but disappear when something (a party at a popular girl's house) or someone "better" (a crush) comes along. Friends count on each other *all* the time, not just when it's convenient. Be the girl your friends can truly count on.

...remember important friend events

Some things might be really important to you but aren't worth a pile of beans to anyone else. And vice versa when it comes to your friends. That's not unusual, but it's key to respect what your friend values, even if it just seems like sentimental silliness to you. Maybe you don't give two hoots about her parents' anniversary, but, for her family it's a big event and she needs your help putting together the perfect present. If you're truly busy and can't help her make that

memory-album, offer some creative insight, like suggesting she include some of the quotes she's been collecting. She'll really appreciate it if she feels you understand that it's important to her. And this rule doesn't just apply to annual dates. If your bud is majorly stressing over a test she's been studying for, wait for her by her locker. Ask her how it went, give her a bear hug and remind her that, no matter what, she did her best. Paying attention to things that are important to your bud shows that you really care about her.

...make friendship a priority

Sometimes it feels like you're being stretched and pulled in a zillion different directions. Everyone feels the pressure when their to-do list feels more like a to-do-*to-me* list— school responsibilities, family stuff, teams, clubs and, yes, friends. But even when you're crazed with three hours of homework, helping with dinner dishes and doing your laundry so you don't have to wear yesterday's Underoos, if your friend really needs you, you should give her some time. Sounds impossible, but that's what being a friend is all about. Remember, you're not the only one with exams, boy troubles and big-time beauty bummers. If your probs spiral out fall off track and "candy-coat" the truth. Sometimes friends candy-coat with the best of intentions. Maybe you want to protect her feelings, keep her from worrying too much, or avoid creating an awkward moment. Sounds admirable. But consider this: Let's say your bud is planning to sport a micro-mini and tummy-bearing tube top the first day of school. She's clearly psyched about her gear but when she models it for you, you cringe —the look is totally inappropriate for school. To save her feelings, you might be tempted to give her the thumbs up and say, "Woo-hoo! Look at you, girl. That outfit is smokin'!" But that's the easy way out. As her true-blue, it's up to you to be real, especially if she asks for your opinion! That doesn't mean you have to be harsh. A nice, "Sister, I love you, and I love the look you're going for. But, I sorta think the mini, the tube top, the glitter, and the chandelier earrings are a bit much for school. Hey! Why not wear that mini with that cute button-down blouse and your new denim jacket instead?" Sometimes, seeing things from a friend's per-spective is just what Dr. Fashion ordered. Chances are, she'll dig your

of control, chill a bit and think about what's really important. Have you asked your BFF about her day? Did you promise to lend her your boots tonight but got so wrapped up in trying to flat iron your hair that you forgot? It's OK if you're the type to make it public knowledge when you're stressed to the gills. Just make sure your friendship doesn't get swept away in the tidal wave. Because you can bet on this: Sometime, sooner or later, you'll need her to drop it all for you.

...honor honesty

Honesty might seem like a friendship no-brainer. But it's easy for friends to suggestions and will surely come to you next time she needs an honest opinion. Think about it—if you had a piece of lettuce caught between your teeth and your BFF said you looked fab, you'd be pretty bummed once you caught a glimpse of your salad-baring smile. If telling your friend the truth is uncomfortable, because sometimes it is, tell her anyway. Say something like this: "It's hard for me to tell you this, but I want to be honest with you."

...make her feel like a million bucks

Obvious friendship fact: Friends like each other. Don't forget that! When you like someone, what do you do? You compliment her—when you mean it, of course. Love the sparkly top your friend bought for the dance? Tell her she looks totally fabulous! You get excited for her. When she makes the hockey team, make sure she knows you're really psyched! And don't forget to catch the games when you can. You should remind her that she's awesome even if she's not feeling so hot about something. Good buds dole out lots of compliments and rally for each other. She is your cheer-leader, and you are hers.

...stick by her when the chips are down

Ever feel like nothing is going your way? Admittedly, some of those times might be your own doing (like not preparing for a test, which means getting a D in social studies), and sometimes they're no one's fault (the snotty girls decided it's your day to be humiliated). When you're down, the last thing you need is to be kicked again. A friend will help you up even if it means getting a little messy. A popular boy at school has found it sporty to call your friend names? Would sticking up for her throw you into the line of fire? Probably, but so what? Step up. She needs you. Stick by her no matter what, and the friend-ship will always stay tight.

Quiz

What's Your Friendship Personality?

Fabulous ways to bond with your buds and make your friendships fun.

Being friends forever takes effort, and there's no magic formula for friendship glue. There is no magic formula for perfect friendships either. But by identifying and understanding your friend's and your own personality types, you can ensure strong BFF bonds. Take this quiz to determine your personality type, marking your answers on a piece of paper. Then ask your friend to take the quiz. No asking what the other person answered—honesty counts! Add up your quiz responses to see which personality type each of you is. Then keep reading to discover important stuff on how to keep the friendship clicking.

1 **You're throwing your annual bash in two weeks. You…**

a: have every last detail, from the tunes to the soda selection, accounted for on your party checklist.

have everybody who is anybody clamoring to be on your guest list.

c: have your mom take over. She's the best at making food, decorating, the whole deal.

d: just hope people show up.

2 **You get easily annoyed with anyone who is...**

a: unpredictable.

b: boring.

c: indecisive.

 insensitive.

3 **You've just been elected to serve on the Student Council. Naturally, you are the...**

a: treasurer. Show me the money!

☆ social committee chair. You're all about planning stuff like pep rallies, dances and fundraisers.

c: President. Need we say more?

d: school ambassador. You are the ideal mediator, and everyone trusts you.

4 **Your sister asks for your worldly advice on the benefits of hot pink lip gloss. You...**

a: carefully think about it before answering.

b: respond immediately—your first thoughts tend to be the best ones.

c: give her your wisdom. After all, who is more worldly than you?

★ are sure not to hurt her feelings but tell her the truth—hot pink just isn't her color.

5 **Your motto would have to be, "It's not whether you win or lose, it's...**

a: how you play the game."

b: how you look when you're playing!"

c: how you win."

☆ teamwork that counts!"

6 **When choosing your clothes for school, you dress...**

a: for the weather. You hate to be too cold or hot.

☆ **b** to impress. You intend to make a fashion statement.

c: for success. You have a no-nonsense style.

d: for comfort. If it feels good, you wear it.

7 **During lunch time, you're busy...**

a: finishing your homework for tomorrow.

b: catching up on the latest gossip.

☆ scoping out plans for the upcoming weekend.

d: making friends with a new girl.

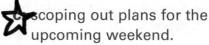

Mostly A's O   THE THINKER

You're a perfectionist, and that's not a bad thing! You don't necessarily need things done your way; you need them done the *right* way. You have high expectations of yourself, your friends and your relationships. You're also less likely to do something that could hurt someone you care about because you always think long and hard before you do or say anything. After a friend fight, *you* are the one tossing and turning over what went wrong. You like to keep things under control, because that's how you can relax and have fun. Cool.

Mostly B's 3   ★THE SOCIALIZER★

Take a quick glance at your datebook. Any empty space in sight? Nope! Not for a social butterfly like you! You've got a schedule full of fun. You don't merely take center stage, you *are* center stage. Your life is filled with praise and compliments, and the limelight is your favorite place to be. And it is through no small effort of your own—you earn the attention you receive. You're friendly, spontaneous, and enthusiastic about everything. Even if you're not the one to throw the party, you are the one who's guaranteed to be invited!

Mostly C's \   THE DOMINATOR

You like to be in control, but that doesn't necessarily mean you want to be the center of attention. In the movie of life, you're the producer rather than the leading lady. You're confident, independent and a total go-getter. There's no time for stress in your life. You're a problem solver—and a quick one at that! Ah, but with your efficient style comes impatience. Friends know to stay out of your way when you have somewhere to be.

Mostly D's 3   THE RELATER

In a time of need, you're a friend indeed. Whether it's a shoulder to cry on or a hug to give, you are most definitely on your friends' A-Lists. Loyalty could be your nickname! You want what's best for you and your buds, and you work hard to help maintain harmony. You can be a bit soft-spoken because you hate to take sides. You refuse to rock the boat and tend to sway with the status quo. But, hey, change can be good.

Your Flourishing Friendship...

You are: DOMINATOR / Your bud is: SOCIALIZER

Things often work out well for the two of you. You're the girl who makes it all happen—deciding what parties you guys will attend or which matinee to hit. Your bud, the Socializer, is happy to follow your direction as long as her social life is brimming with excitement.

School brings changes, so be patient with your Socializer bud. She's apt to spend time hanging with lots of classmates and, of course, getting the latest dish. Stay involved with all your activities 'til your super-social pal comes flittering by for your companionship and guidance.

You are: DOMINATOR / Your bud is: RELATER

Your bud, the Relater, is often your saving grace. Being the control-hungry girl that you are, you can rub people the wrong way. However, your loyal bud comes to the rescue, smoothing things over and keeping everyone happy! The Relater isn't as opinionated as you are, so she balances you well.

Your friend is so appreciated for her friendly ways. She's stoked to be in the mix of things. Set aside time in your day planner to listen to her latest escapades and feelings, and your friendship will continue to rock.

You are: DOMINATOR / Your bud is: THINKER

While the two of you are both perfectionists, you have very different styles. You are a person of action, often working by trial-and-error. Your friend, on the other hand, tends to think carefully before making a single move. The Thinker will map out all possibilities on paper before jumping into anything.

So, in many ways, the two of you are actually opposites. But that's OK since friendships often thrive on differences. To keep this relationship perfect for both of you, give her time to ponder things. You both tend to sway away from your emotions, so take the time to tell each other how lucky you are to be buds.

You are: **DOMINATOR**/Your bud is: **DOMINATOR**

Oh, boy...Here comes trouble! As buds, you two are the dynamic duo. When you're on the same wavelength, the two of you are unstoppable. But when the chips are down, everyone better hit the deck! It's head-to-head combat, and neither of you has any intention to wave that white flag of surrender.

You two spend many, many hours debating about anything and everything. To the Dominator, it's not always (or only) about who is right or wrong, but who wins the fight! However, if you really value the friendship, you'll need to take time out from the friendly fire to get in touch with your emotional sides—something you both rarely do.

You are: **SOCIALIZER**/Your bud is: **THINKER**

You and the Thinker might as well have come from different planets. Your bud is as ultra-cautious as you are impulsive. You'd often like to give your bud a kick in the caboose to get her moving. Meanwhile, the Thinker would like to paste you to a chair so you'll sit still for a sec! You balance out for each other what otherwise might be a life of extremes.

You each take pleasure in different activities. You're into school dances, and she's into chilling at the coffee shop. Take turns—one weekend take your friend to the hottest soirées, and the next weekend hang at all her favorite haunts. Appreciate each other for what you both bring to this great relationship. Opposites really do attract!

You are: **SOCIALIZER**/Your bud is: **RELATER**

You're like a butterfly. You flit from event to event, enjoying every minute. Life is a social engagement, and you wouldn't have it any other way. However, reliability is not your strong point. This is where your friend the Relater steps in. She's often there to remind you of your responsibilities and obligations.

Your bud likes to hang out at parties, but for her it's not all about being seen. It's more about the friends she gets to catch up with at get-togethers. Don't forget the greatest friends are those who are around even when there's no party to be found! Let her know how important she is to you as a friend, not just as a social sidekick.

You are: **SOCIALIZER**/Your bud is: **DOMINATOR**

You two have a great relationship. The Dominator fills your social calendar, and you happily go along for the ride. The exact opposite holds true for your bud—she's the woman behind the wheel. She's into making the plans, and you're into executing them with her.

The Dominator thinks there's more to life than parties. She has a plan for her life's success. For a Socializer, it wouldn't hurt to tag along and shadow her in her endeavors. You'll learn from her, and she'll love having charming you around.

You are: **SOCIALIZER**/Your bud is: **SOCIALIZER**

Wow! You two are a party on the move. Never a dull moment. You rarely take time to breathe, much less battle. But when you do fight, the scenes you make are worthy of Academy Awards. Oh, the drama!

The trick to friendship success for you two social butterflies is to make sure to leave enough time for school and fun! Socializers tend to find it's difficult to buckle down. Why not think of a way to make a party out of doing your homework? If anyone can do that, it's you two!

You are: **THINKER**/Your bud is: **DOMINATOR**

Let's face it—you guys don't have a lot in common. While the Dominator likes to be in charge, you are more concerned with every nitty-gritty detail! Your tendency toward perfection leads you to move at a slower pace. Meanwhile, your friend is quick to act and even quicker to run over those particulars you painstakingly work on getting just right.

Is it possible for you to be friends? Actually, yes. With a little compromise, you might find that a faster clip is exhilarating and fulfilling. And the Dominator should undoubtedly see how nice it is to take the time to smell the peonies!

You are: THINKER/Your bud is: SOCIALIZER

If two people ever came from opposite ends of the spectrum, it's definitely the two of you. While you are extremely detail-oriented and consumed by perfection, your best bud is driven by emotion and flies by the seat of her jeans. It doesn't matter how or why the two of you got to be such great friends, so don't waste time trying to figure that out!

You've probably analyzed your Socializer friend down to the last molecule. And you probably already know how to make this friendship a successful one. Take a tip from your Socializer friend, however, and try not to sweat the small details. The big picture of life looks bigger and brighter that way!

You are: THINKER/Your bud is: RELATER

Out of all the personality types, you two are the most laid-back. Harmony is an important part of both your lives—you're on an intellectual level and the Relater's on an emotional one. This is a great match.

Your relationship is always even-keeled. To spice it up, give the brain a break, and go for an occasional girls' night. Rent sappy movies, microwave some popcorn, and get in touch with your emotional side. Your Relater bud can help you in that department!

You are: THINKER/Your bud is: THINKER

If there were a solution to world hunger, you two would discover it! It might take a hundred years but, through your diligence, you'd eventually feed the whole planet. You both have busy, busy minds, and that's a great thing. She's got her issues to ponder, and you've got yours. Together, you're a brainiac tag team!

But there's more to life than graph paper and textbooks, so get out from behind those desks and go enjoy yourselves! Friendships flourish when buds do many different activities together, not just hit the books or worry in sync about an exam for a class you share. Go out, and maybe use your big brains to woo some cute boys.

You are: **RELATER**/Your bud is: **DOMINATOR**

You're a team player, and your best bud is a born leader. When you guys are together, everyone wants to be on your team! What better set-up could there possibly be? She makes the plans, and you keep the peace!

However, as a Dominator, your friend sometimes gets a little too caught up in the fast pace of things, so occasionally remind her to slow down for a breather. Grab hold of the reins once in a while to give her a break from all that planning and scheduling. Let her know you like her for more than her organizational skills. You dig her softer, more sentimental side, as well—when she shows it!

You are: **RELATER**/Your bud is: **SOCIALIZER**

You two like to be in joy mode. "Don't worry, be happy" is your mutual mantra. However, while you are in tune with the needs and wants of the people around you, your Socializer bud is largely concerned with herself. Relators need to ground their Socializer friends. And Socializers need to pep up their Relator buds.

You two rarely get into a tiff. But when you do, it shouldn't be too difficult for you to pull your swinging Socializer down a notch from her self-centeredness. After all, as the Relater, you know what makes people tick. Just be sure to take a stance and not be bowled over by her wild ways.

You are: **RELATER**/Your bud is: **THINKER**

You and your bud are pretty much on an even keel. Peace and happiness are important to both of you. However, while you are quick to overlook faults, the Thinker can be overly critical. Because of this, you might have more friends than she does. And she's probably perfectly happy just having you as one of her few friends.

Neither of you has a mean bone in your body—that's why you make such great friends. However, your Thinker friend might sometimes be overwhelmed by your shows of affection, so give her some space. Never fear—she's definitely your friend for life. She appreciates you for your own brand of thoughtfulness!

You are: RELATER/
Your bud is: RELATER

You and your fellow Relater bud probably have one of the greatest friendships around. You're extremely loyal to one another and are always available when the other is in need. If ever in a tiff, you come out as even better friends.

Your friendship will endure as long as you're honest and don't try to protect each other's feelings. It's OK to disagree and have dissenting opinions. It doesn't make you a lesser friend. Once you are able to stop trying to always please each other, you'll build an even greater friend-ship.

Put those feelings into words

You always tell your BFF how special and cool she is. But why not write her a poem so she can look at it and be reminded daily? "Whoa," you say, "I'm no Emily Dickinson." Never fear—your BFF Poem-o-matic is here:

Line 1: Your friend's full formal name

Line 2: Four words that describe your friend

Line 3: "Lover of…" one thing or idea

Line 4: "Believes in…"

Line 5: "Who gave," or, "Who said" (a quote)

Line 6: Your friend's nickname

Here's an example:

Britney Jean Spears

Hip, princess, trustworthy, sweet

Lover of dance

Believes in the essence of music

Who said, "This job isn't all the glamour that you see on TV. It's not like that at all. You have to love what you are doing and you have to love to sing."

Pinky

The insiders club

What really makes a friendship cooler than every other relationship you have? Endless inside jokes? A secret language? Or those silly nicknames that stick like glue? Here are some tips on how to morph any friendship into a closer one.

Laugh out Loud

If you hung out with Brandy and Paige, both 11, you might mistake 'em for Rachel and Monica hamming it up on *Friends*. These best friends *never* stop laughing, and it never gets old. Says Paige, "Wherever we go, we crack each other up—and the people around us, even our teachers!" Brandy says, "We have the most fun when we tease each other. It's all in good fun, and we never say anything hurtful." Having things to laugh about keeps BFFs close.

Secret Speak

Want a secret language? Make one up! To make a special language for note passing, create your characters using shapes to match existing letters. For example, "A" could be an apple or three diagonal lines—it's up to you—and so on for the rest of the alphabet. Create a "key," and make sure you both have copies. Cara, 10, says, "I use my second language when e-mailing my best friend because I share an account with my family." Just make sure your pesky bro doesn't get his mitts on your decoder key.

Pick a Nick

Sometimes, goofy nicknames are just the glue needed to bond a friendship. Without even realizing it, Erica, 12, started calling her BFF "Cookie," because her BFF loves Oreo cookies. And Erica's obsession with VW Beetles earned her the nickname "Bug." Serena, 11, says this: "Nicknames are fun, and they're the best when you're passing notes and don't want to be ID'd!" Who'd ever guess Serena is also known as "Boo," "Babe," and "Basket-case"? Only her BFF knows her multiple IDs!

Friends Are Friends

No doubt about it, having a best friend is a blast. Sharing belly laughs and "just between the two of us" moments bring friends closer. Sharing secrets and cryptic notes makes a friendship super strong. But keep those secrets under wraps—the friendship will be that much sweeter. Cross our hearts!

start your own Friendship Traditions

Don't you just love traditions? From making Valentines on Valentine's Day, to watching fireworks on the Fourth of July, to eating turkey at Thanksgiving, traditions bring people together. Wouldn't it be great to start your own traditions with your friends? You and your best buds can create some totally new activities to forever enjoy at any special time of the year. With this list of fun-with-friends tradition ideas, you and your friends can make your own special things to share together each year.

January
Throw an after-holiday swap meet

Not into the itchy cardigan your aunt gave you but love hand-held games, and your friend loves big wooly sweaters, but she got doubles on a Game Boy? Swap! Your bud hates white chocolate (and got a whole box), but you love the creamy sweets. Why not trade her the cool ponytail holders you no longer need, thanks to your new short 'do? Make your swap meet the after-season event of the year!

February
Celebrate Valentine's Day with an all-girl gathering

Grab your best buds and have a love fest. Make homemade Valentine cards and toss in some little candy message hearts! Fill out Valentines to your girlfriends, guy friends, fave teachers, and your crushes. You don't have to do a thing but sign your name and tuck a few candy hearts in the mini envelope. There will be so much love spreading on V-Day that everyone will be tickled pink.

march
Have a toy drive

Do some spring-cleaning and get together some toys to donate to a local children's hospital. Get buds to bring those plastic ponies they're ready to part with or a new toy that your well-meaning neighbor didn't realize you were too old for. Wrap the gifts to look brand spanking new. Hint: Don't forget batteries for toys that need them.

april
Enjoy a rainy day movie marathon

Devote an entire rainy day to watching some feel-good friend flicks like *Now and Then, Crossroads,* or *Clueless.* Have each friend bring their favorite movie-time treat, like Sno-Caps or Raisinets, and you supply the tubs of popcorn. This can also be a great time to catch up on friendly gossip with the gang. Just remember to keep the talking to a minimum. Shush! People are trying to watch the movie.

may
Beautify Mother Nature

Get in touch with your school or neighborhood park, and see if they'd like some help beautifying their landscape. If they already have a flower planting crew, ask your parents if they'd love a little garden of color in your backyard. Then gather some buds who aren't afraid of getting dirty, and have them bring their favorite flower to the soirée. Borrow some gardening tools from the 'rents or neighbors, and get planting. Organize your garden as a group to show every flower at its best.

june
Cater to your whims

Gather friends for supper, and arrange it so everybody brings a dish from a specific country. For example, the country chosen is Italy, so someone brings a pasta dish, another an antipasto salad, someone else garlic bread, another friend Italian pastries, and so on. Whoever hosts the get together, chooses the country.

july
Be all-American

Show your spirit by supporting your community's local sports team. It doesn't matter whether it's a major league baseball game or just your younger bro's little league team. Grab your buds and cheer the team on to V-I-C-T-O-R-Y! Who cares if they win or lose, have everyone over to celebrate with a backyard BBQ. Don't forget dessert. The day can't be complete without some homemade apple pie and vanilla ice cream—*mmm!*

august
Prepare a back-to-school beauty bonanza

It's your last chance to stay up late before school starts. Invite all the gals over for a sleepover spa party. Assign each girl a task. Who's got a gazillion bottles of glittery nail polish? She's your manicurist. Who's really into mud masks and skin treatments? She'll do the facials. Practice make-up techniques, and pick out the right shades and colors for everyone. You'll be glam goddesses ready to go back-to-school!

september
Spread good cheer to the elderly

When school starts and you're superbusy, it's always good to take time out for your friends—and others. Have you ever seen a nursing home resident perk up when she gets a visitor? Just an hour out of your day can bring so much joy to a senior. You and your pals can take cookies to break the ice. And remember to bring your best jokes, tap dance routines, magic tricks, and smiles. You'll have the most enthusiastic audience ever.

october
Have a homemade Halloween

Wanna be the most popular gal in the neighborhood—that is, with all the little kiddies? You will be when you and your gal pals set up the most disgusting, gross, super-scary haunted house for the kids in your area. Dress up as witches, goblins, and ghosts, and lure the children through your haunted house. Set up jars filled with peeled grapes and Jell-O, but tell the kids they're eyeballs and brains. Now remember, it can't be too frightening or some of the kids may get so freaked they never come back. And wouldn't that just be a shame....

november
Start a memory box

Thanksgiving may mean turkey, but it also can mean time to spend with your BFF! Decorate a shoebox collage-style with magazine clippings, cut-out paper flowers, stickers, glitter, whatever. Then, you and your bud write down a list of your best and silliest moments of the year, plus what you're most thankful for. On the back of the list, tape a photo of the two of you together and place it in the box. Vow not to open the box until next year, when you'll do the same thing all over again. After a few years, you'll have a spectacular history of your friendship!

december
Volunteer at a soup kitchen

Get in the holiday spirit by helping others who are less fortunate. Instead of trading gifts, why don't you and your BFF spend a little time this holiday season volunteering at a soup kitchen or homeless shelter, doling out warm and tasty meals to the poor and needy? Unwrapping presents can be great, but giving back will make you feel even better.

Best Friends

Chapter 3

Wanted: a Best Friend Forever

Even though your buds are super great, you want someone to share your deepest secrets, know exactly what you're thinking even before you say it, and be able to call ten times a day without being annoying. You want a best friend. If you could have that, you wouldn't need a whole bunch of other friends, right? Well maybe—or maybe not. Keep reading.

Groups Can Be Great

Newsflash! Lots of girls actually don't have one best friend—and they like it that way. The truth is, having one best bud can be limiting.

Molly, 12, used to have one best friend but decided it wasn't working for her. "My friend and I were having problems, and I couldn't figure out why," she remembers. "Then I realized I was so caught up in being another girl's 'best friend' that I forgot about my other friends." The benefits of having many good buds rather than one super tight one are bountiful—more phone pals, more clothes to borrow, more shoulders to cry on, more study buddies, more fun!

Star Search

If you still think you're in dire need of a sister soul mate, ask yourself some questions: Are your friends giving you enough emotional support? Do you feel left out all the time, or just when it's time to pick lab partners? Figure out what's bugging you. Once you uncover why you yearn for one special BFF, the situation should become crystal clear. Maybe you'll realize you've already got fabulous friends, you just needed a confidante. Or (gulp!), maybe you'll realize your friends aren't so right for you, after all. If you choose to continue your BFF quest, here are some things to ponder:

45

- Are you up for commitment? Best friends take work! Are you up to it? Are you able to be ultra-supportive? Ready to deal with potential pitfalls and best-friend-level dilemmas? If you answer a hearty, "Yes!" then go for it and find yourself a BFF.

- Have you looked closely at the girls you already hang with? Who in your group always makes you smile? Who loves Josh Hartnett as much as you do? Who goes out of her way to make sure you're invited to every party? If one girl stands out a bit above the rest, maybe your BFF is in plain sight!

- BFF material isn't right under your nose? You might have to branch out beyond the confines of comfort and familiarity. Sit at a different lunch table one day a week. Join a new club. Take an art class outside of school. See if there's a youth group you can check out. Be brave. Get out there and meet new gals!

- Are you trying too hard? You can't force a friendship, especially a best friendship. "Picking" a best friend isn't like shopping for the season's newest jeans. Deep friendships develop over time and through shared experiences. They don't just—poof!—happen overnight. So be patient, and don't push it.

The Bottom Line

If you still feel like you're missing out, please stop obsessing. You could find the perfect BFF when you least expect it. Or you might stumble across so many potential best friends that you're back to square one. Having gobs of good friends, but not one best friend, isn't such a bad thing. In fact, it's quite the opposite. By having bunches of buds, you have more friends to count on and call on all the time. Truth be told, "BFF" is really just a label anyway. And, hey, whoever said the Friend in BFF can't be plural? Best *Friends* Forever. Hmm, nice ring to it!

Quiz

Do You Really Know Your BFF?

"**M**y best friend and I are like two peas in a pod," you say. "I know her better than she knows herself," your BFF claims of you. But do you really know your best friend as well as you think? Does she truly know you? Here's one way to find out! Grab two pieces of paper and two pens. Answer each section about your best bud. Have her do the same for you, and then swap papers for scoring. Give one point for each right answer and add up the points to see if you really are BFFs. (Psst! Don't read the scoring analysis at the end of the quiz until after you're done scoring each other.) OK, have fun!

part one
Would She or Wouldn't She?

Write "true" or "false" for each statement according to how you think your best bud would behave in each of the situations below.

1 If the school bully forced some younger kid to eat moldy pizza on a dare, my friend would be the first to stand up for the under- classman and stop the fiasco.

○ true ○ false

2 She'd tell you if the skirt you had on was totally cheesy and wrong—*before* you left the house.

○ true ○ false

3 If she found a cool necklace lying on the sidewalk, she'd say, "Score!" and clasp it around her neck, claiming it as her own.

○ true ○ false

4 She'd tell a "little white lie" to your parents—and hers—if it meant protecting you from getting grounded for a month.

○ true ○ false

5 She'd peek over her shoulder at your history test, if you weren't careful with your paper.

○ true ○ false

6 The morning after a sleepover, if your mom announced that it was time to clean up the house, she'd be out the door before you could blink away your eye crust.

○ true ○ false

part TWO

Pick Your Friend's Favorites

In each category, check every item your best bud could never live without.

Accessories:

- ○ Cool hats
- ○ Glasses
- ○ Earrings
- ○ Trendy necklaces
- ○ Big wrap belts
- ○ Rings
- ○ Bracelets
- ○ Toe rings

Clothes:

- ○ Jeans
- ○ Sweats
- ○ Skirts
- ○ Dresses
- ○ T-shirts
- ○ Tank tops
- ○ Anything clean

Fun Things to Do:

- ○ Shopping
- ○ Museums
- ○ Walks in the park
- ○ Talking on the phone
- ○ Picnics
- ○ Surfing online
- ○ Movies

Food:

- ○ Pizza
- ○ Burrito
- ○ Spaghetti
- ○ Veggie burger
- ○ Candy, cookies, ice cream
- ○ Chips, dips, and other snack foods

School Subject:

- ○ English
- ○ Math
- ○ Science
- ○ Social studies
- ○ Languages
- ○ P.E.
- ○ Lunch

Hobbies:

- ○ Sports
- ○ Reading
- ○ Dance
- ○ Musical instruments
- ○ Art projects

Shoes:

- ○ Sneakers
- ○ Chunky boots
- ○ Strappy sandals
- ○ Flip-flops
- ○ Slippers

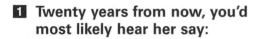

Circle the letter next to the ONE choice from each question that best fits your friend.

1 Twenty years from now, you'd most likely hear her say:

a: "The rainforest is safe now."

b: "That's Madam President to you, Bub."

c: "I want to thank the Academy."

d: "Would you like fries with that?"

2 Her future address is in:

a: the middle of nowhere.

b: smack in the middle of a big city.

c: right here.

d: a country you need an atlas to find.

3 Her first car is going to be:

a: a Jeep.

b: a Volkswagen Beetle.

c: an electric car to take her to those few places her mountain bike can't.

d: anything that has four wheels and a radio.

4 If she could redo her bedroom, it would have:

a: a four-poster bed, lots of pillows, frilly sheets.

b: a futon, bookshelf, and her CDs.

c: wall-to-wall band posters.

d: a really, *really* big closet with a computerized accessorizing system.

5 Her perfect night is:

a: hanging out at a fun party.

b: renting a movie.

c: heading out for a sunset hike.

d: meeting lots of friends at a diner or at the mall.

6 Her dream boy would:

a: hike mountains, save whales, recycle.

b: be captain of the football team, baseball team, and soccer team.

c: be super cute, well-known, and funny.

d: be mushy, write poems for her, call everyday.

7 She'll name her first daughter:

a: after her mom.

b: after her favorite literary heroine.

c: after you.

d: after her favorite movie star.

your HeLP!

My new BFF feels excluded from all the fun. I always invite her to parties and movies, but her mom never lets her come along. How can I include my BFF when her mother is so super strict?

If a BFF's mom has never met me, I'd make a point to introduce myself. Then, I would ask my mom to talk to her mom—maybe they could reach an agreement as to what's allowed and what's not. Sometimes, moms have to talk to other moms!

—Shaina, 10

My BFF's parents were very strict. I'd invited my BFF skating and to plays, but she could never go. I had to invite my other friends. So I asked her parents if we could hang at her house. She no longer feels left out, and her parents are less strict.

—Alaina, 10

Nicely ask her mom what she's allowed to do—and then do that! If she's not allowed to watch PG-13 movies, go see a G or PG movie with her. But don't feel guilty about seeing PG-13 movies with another friend!

—Shannon, 11

Tell your BFF you aren't trying to exclude her—it has nothing to do with her personality. Suggest she explain to her mom how she feels. Maybe you could reassure her mom that everything will be OK, too.

—Laura, 10

part Four

In a Perfect World

For each of the following questions, check one celebrity you believe your friend would choose in each situation.

1 If she could trade places with one of the following famous celebs, she'd choose:

a: Mia Hamm.

b: Britney Spears.

c: Oprah Winfrey.

d: Sarah Michelle Gellar.

2 She'd most love to have a date with:

a: Josh Hartnett.

b: Justin Timberlake.

c: Prince William.

d: Lil' Bow Wow.

3 She would most like to raid the closet of:

a: Jennifer Lopez.

b: Mandy Moore.

c: Pink.

d: Alicia Keys.

4 **If she could trade her mom for a mom on TV, she would pick:**

a: Reba Hart on *Reba.*

b: Annie Camden on *7th Heaven.*

c: Lorelai Gilmore on *Gilmore Girls.*

d: She wouldn't trade her mom for anyone else, even for a quiz!

5 **If she could star in the remake of any movie it would be:**

a: *Save the Last Dance.*

b: *Clueless.*

c: *Breakfast at Tiffany's.*

d: *Titanic.*

YOUR HELP!

My new BFF always calls my house past midnight. I get in trouble! How can I stop the late-night calls?

If your BFF doesn't realize you get in trouble for it, make sure she understands the rule. If she still calls, she doesn't respect you or your parents. If your friend doesn't respect a simple rule, then she's not a best friend.
—Sarah, 12

I'd set certain times for my friend to call. One night, she can call me at a certain time. The next night, I can call her at a certain time. Or she could e-mail me any time of night!
—Francesca, 12

Unlike your BFF, you actually like to sleep and so do your parents. To stop the wake-up calls, kindly but firmly tell her you like when she calls, but not after 10 p.m.
—Michelle, 11

Because you've explained that she's causing trouble, maybe it's time to tell your parents. Have them pick up the phone and remind her of the rules. If she's a real friend, she'll understand.
—Madison, 10

I like to go to bed early, so I constantly deal with this problem. Maybe your friend doesn't realize how strict your parents are. Make sure she knows your phone privileges could be taken away totally.
—Mackenzie, 11

part Five
Loves and Hates

Finish each of the following sentences:

Her favorite television show of all time is...

_____

She is most likely to spend her allowance on...

_____

Her biggest pet peeve is...

_____

Her dream vacation would be spent in...

_____

She's crazy to meet...

_____

The one beauty product she can't live without is...

_____

The quality she most loves about you (her BFF) is...

_____

part Six
In a Nutshell

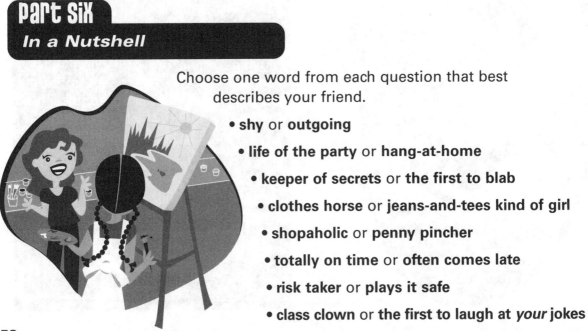

Choose one word from each question that best describes your friend.

- **shy** or **outgoing**
- **life of the party** or **hang-at-home**
- **keeper of secrets** or **the first to blab**
- **clothes horse** or **jeans-and-tees kind of girl**
- **shopaholic** or **penny pincher**
- **totally on time** or **often comes late**
- **risk taker** or **plays it safe**
- **class clown** or **the first to laugh at _your_ jokes**

Scoring: Add It Up!

Swap papers, and give one point for each answer your friend got right about you—and you got right about your friend. Add up the points, then check below to see if your friend totally gets you—and if you get her—or if you need to get to know each other a little better.

31-40 points:
Identical Twins

You two aren't just of the same pod, you're practically the same pea. It's awesome that you've found your truest of buds. Knowing each other so well means you can really help each other in times of need and social planning. Instead of guessing what's best for each other, you rely on really understanding what the other wants and needs. You're lucky, but don't forget there are lots of other great girls out there, too, so don't tune yourselves out completely to the rest of the world.

11-20 points:
Room for Improvement

You gals have to clue in a little. Just because you didn't score highly on this quiz doesn't mean you have to trash the friendship, but best friends should know a *little* more about each other. If you like and trust each other, make more one-on-one time. Go for a hike, hang in the backyard, or just crash on the floor and chat. You don't have to force bonding by spilling your guts, but try to open up. Share some of your thoughts, and experiences. Use this quiz to get you started, and remember, learning about each other is supposed to be fun!

21-30 points:
Closest of Companions

Just because you're not attached at the hip doesn't mean you're not good friends. You're obviously in sync with each other and enjoy talking about stuff that's important to you. Best friends don't always have to be the oracle of each other's lives to be true BFFs, and you both may be happiest exactly where you are in your friendship. If you aspire to know more about each other, finding out is as easy as talking about the questions on this quiz!

1-10 points:
Missing the Boat

Yikes! Did you take this quiz with a stranger? Put simply, friendship takes effort. Try following the advice in "Room for Improvement" (above). When on the listening end, pay close attention to your friend, ask questions and make an effort to truly understand her. Be sure she's doing the same for you. You may have to remind each other, but, hey, the friendship can only grow. If it doesn't, you may have to find some new friend who's more willing to want to know who you are and what you're all about.

BFF Boredom Busters

You and your BFF are bored to tears. You've sat through every feature at the 26-screen Cineplex. Going to the swim club everyday isn't exactly a splash. And it's not like you can book two tickets for an exotic European vacation. No problem! There's still plenty you two can do. All you need is creativity and motivation to have a lot of fun.

For Sporty BFFS:

Sure school sports are fun, but why not join a neighborhood league? Go with an old fave or try something new—water-basketball, Frisbee, golf, or scavenger-hunt hikes. Check your local rec center for ideas.

For Business BFFs:

Come up with some hot ideas for making cold hard cash. You two could try dog-walking, serving at parties, helping neighbors with painting or lawn work. Once you have an idea and goals, make up a funky flyer and print copies to distribute.

For Crafty BFFs:

You can get art supplies for dirt cheap—glitter, stencils, clay, fabric. Use your imagination. Prefer to follow directions? There are plenty of kits and craft books on the market. Even better, sign up for an art class or check out a do-it-yourself pottery place.

For Adventurous BFFs:

One day a week, do something you've never done before. Try fly fishing, yoga, or a first-aid course. Turn your yard into a mini-golf course using cans for holes (no digging up the lawn). Make it more challenging by putting down obstacles. Up the ante by saying the loser takes the winner out for ice cream.

For Giving BFFs:

Volunteering is where it's at! Call a volunteer outreach program in your area and ask what services are needed. Even if the project isn't exactly a day at the beach, you and your BFF will have done something meaningful.

Friendship Triangles

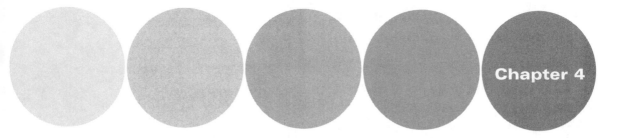

Chapter 4

What to Do When Two's Company, but Three's a Crowd

Kim and Holly have been the best of friends since third grade. They walked to elementary school together, swapped clothes and had sleepovers on the weekends. Then last year, when they hit middle school, something changed. The formerly inseparable duo began splitting apart at the seams.

"Kim and I were like sisters," Holly, 11, explains. "But in middle school, she acted like a different person. She got her hair cut all crazy, acquired a wacky wardrobe and acted like a complete stranger." Why the sudden transformation?

Kim, 11, says she needed a change. "Holly and I were like twins," Kim says. "It was fun, but when I met Melanie, I started thinking, 'Hey, there's no rule that says we have to be clones.' I also realized I don't have to go through life with only one good friend.

"Melanie introduced me to all sorts of new people. She liked cool music, and she didn't cling to me like Holly did. I guess that having one best friend for so many years just got a little boring—and even annoying. Holly thought my friendship with Melanie would leave her in the dust, but I wanted all three of us to be friends. You know—the more, the merrier."

Kim and Holly are learning to work out their friendship triangle. When it's good, it's an equally balanced triangle. One is good to the other is good to the other. Instead of one BFF, there are two, which doubles the benefits of being best friends. Cool.

My BFF is super cool, but none of my other friends like her. I want us all to be friends. Can this work?

Find common interests between them. If they like basketball—set up a game to include all your friends. Who knows? Maybe they'll hit it off.
—*Caroline, 12*

Your buds should respect any other friends you have—or they really aren't good friends. Let them know how cool your BFF is and that they should give her a chance—maybe they'll even gain a new friend.
—*Kelsey, 10*

If she really is a cool friend, stay friends with her no matter what your other friends say. Unfortunately, not everyone gets along. Try to stay friends with everyone, even if you can't all be together.
—*Melissa, 12*

It would be really hurtful to ditch your BFF based on what others think. Ask your group why they dislike her. Try to get the two sides talking, and maybe they'll learn to like each other.
—*Kathleen, 11*

Tell your other friends straight up how you feel. Talk to them about trying to get to know your BFF. If they still hate her, you'll just have to divide your time fairly.
—*Becca, 10*

Odd Girl Out?

The problem with the number three is that it's uneven, so eventually somebody is going to feel left out. If one gal senses she's being pushed away, or the other two girls really are pushing her away, the friendship triangle will weaken and probably stop standing all together. Usually, that person isn't actually being forgotten, it just feels that way.

Let's say two friends grab tacos after studying for a test in a class they share, but the third only "hears" that she was left out of the fiesta. She feels totally dissed. But here's the thing: She's not even in the same class. The study buddies weren't excluding her to be obnoxious, they honestly didn't consider she'd want to sit in on a study session for a class she didn't take. It might sound silly, but those sorts of crossed signals could cause the triangle to topple!

Why It's So Great to Be Three!

It's perfectly natural for pals to seek out new friendships and experiences. So, don't be surprised if another girl comes along who wants to hang with you guys. If you and your best friend are the dynamic duo, that's fab, but don't shut yourselves off to the possibility of meeting a perfect third! You never know!

Seems a candidate for your two-person clique is hanging around the perimeter? Don't freak. Try not to think of the third girl as an enemy invader. Think of her as another friend with whom to share secrets, swap clothes, hang with after school, complain about teachers, and watch movies.

If you don't make her out to be an intruder, she just might be a bonus. She could even make your relationship with your best friend even stronger because she could be a "buffer" to any of the naggy, little peeves you guys have with each other. She could be the voice of reason if things between you and your BFF ever heat up. Not to mention she could be as cool as cool comes.

To reap the benefits of having two BFFs, be yourself—the same groovy gal you've always been. Do your best to keep the lines of communication wide open—if you're feeling slighted, speak up. Don't assume you're being ditched—talk to your friends. News flash: All three of you don't have to do everything together all the time. If two are hanging together, then they're hanging. It doesn't mean they're hanging without the third, get it?

Keeping Jealousy Under Wraps

Stressing about the new girl who's having so much fun with your BFF? Instead of freaking that she's your replacement, entertain the idea of branching out. But we're not going to lie—clearly this isn't as easy as it

sounds. Prepare yourself for a whole bunch of crazy feelings like jealousy, insecurity, or frustration.

Shelley, 12, remembers "throwing a fit" when she thought her best friend Caroline, 12, ditched her for Annie, also, 12. Yet no matter how typical it is for friends to feel jealous, that doesn't mean it hurts any less when you feel like your best bud suddenly has all the time in the world for someone else—and seemingly none for you.

YOUR HELP!

I invite my BFF to go out with me and my other friends, but she never invites me. Or she lies and says she's not going out. Why won't my BFF invite me to hang with her neighborhood friends?

Confront your BFF. Explain that you're hurt when she lies. Tell her you'd like to hang with her and her friends too. She probably doesn't tell you when she's going out because she doesn't want to hurt your feelings.

—*Amanda, 12*

If your BFF lies to you and doesn't seem to want you around, she isn't a true friend. Don't let your BFF's insecurity upset you. Try to hang out with other friends, and focus on the ones you have.

—*Carley, 12*

I don't have friends like that. A true friend is nothing like that—a friend hangs out with you and doesn't lie to you about plans.

—*Evangaline, 10*

If you want to stay friends with your BFF, ask her why she never invites you to go out with her friends. Then ask, "Are you my friend?" If she says, "Yes," hopefully, she'll make some changes. And if she says, "No," find a new BFF.

—*Usai, 10*

This happened to me. Break away. Make the first move. Get to know girls in other groups. Once you break the ice, your bud might realize cliques are immature. Then you two will be able to hang out.

—*Whitney, 12*

"I was such a jerk to Annie when she first started hanging out with Caroline and me," Shelley says. "I used to try to show off to make Annie look bad, but later I found out my Know-It-All act only made me look desperate and bratty."

Caroline agrees: "Shelley was so totally out of control from the first time I had Annie over my house. We laugh about it now, but back then she was totally blown away that my attention was going to Annie. Plus, she was paranoid—always wondering what we were up to when she wasn't around. But we didn't do anything cooler when she wasn't there. And we certainly didn't sit around talking trash about her."

We're not saying don't ever be jealous when a new girl enters the picture. You may feel that way regardless of logic or better judgment. If it helps, write down your feelings, yell at your pillow, or go for a run. Then come back to Planet Reality. Everyone brings something different to a friendship. And just because someone new has grabbed the attention of your BFF, it doesn't mean she's over you and all you bring to the friend-ship. And remember you don't have to like everyone or everything your best friend does.

Making the Triangle Strong

The trick to making a friendship triangle work is for all three girls to feel good about themselves. If one girl lets her jealousy or feelings of insecurity get the best of her, one side of the triangle gets all lopsided and out of whack.

If she feels like she's not good enough for her old friend or like she did something wrong—that's insecurity. And insecurity within any relationship is sure to cause all sorts of drama. She might go from a happy-go-lucky-gal to a sad, paranoid soul and that's no good! It's so important to make sure you and the other legs of the triangle feel confident and secure, or trouble is sure to brew.

Wendy, 10, says she started wondering what was wrong with her when her best friend, Jaime, 10, was spending every weekend with another girl, Sara, 11. "I kept asking myself, 'Did I say something stupid? Did I act like a dork?' I kept comparing myself to Sara. I copied the way she talked and the way she ate—it was pretty dumb."

Wendy felt like she wasn't herself anymore—she was just a mirror of Sara. It wasn't fun to shop, because she just hunted for stuff that looked like Sara's style. It wasn't fun to talk about movies since Sara isn't really

YOUR HELP!

Help! My BFF and I are having a combo birthday bash. I don't like some people she's inviting. How can we settle on the guest list?

Decide if it would totally ruin your party if her friends came. Maybe this would be a good chance for you to get to know some of her friends.
—*Kelsey, 10*

I would enjoy myself even if I didn't like the people invited. Since the party is not only my BFF's, but also mine, she should consider that I have issues with some people. I'd also consider that she might not like everyone I invited. Life's not always fair.
—*Pilar, 12*

Everybody has different personalities. We can't all like the same people. I wouldn't say anything to my BFF because it's only one night. It might hurt her feelings if I did. I would be polite and hang with people I like.
—*Moriah, 10*

I would talk politely to my BFF and ask her to rethink her guest list. If she still invites them, I would still have a good time! When I see these people at the party, I would just smile and wave.
—*Nicole, 10*

It's my BFF's party, too, and I wouldn't want to ruin our fun. I would just stay away from the people I don't like so I could have a good time, like everyone else.
—*Brittany, 11*

into celebs—that meant Wendy pretented not to care about them either. Soon she was miserable. That's when Wendy figured out there was nothing wrong with her: "I hadn't changed, and I realized I was questioning myself for no good reason. I just felt like a loser when Sara came along because she seemed so exciting to Jamie and I was so worried I'd be left out."

Soon afterward, Wendy, Sara and Jaime became really great friends. "After a few weeks of torture, I realized how awesome it is to share things with more than one friend," says Wendy. "I get different advice from Jaime and Sara. And I have another person I can trust."

Loosening the Reins

Here are some words of wisdom from girls who've suffered through the pain of feeling dumped for the new girl in town: Don't treat a friend like she's a possession. You can't force your pal to feel or act a certain way, so trying to won't get you what you want, which is quality time with your friend.

The more you try to hold onto her, the more she'll want to cut loose. (Think of how *you* feel when your parents hold *you* back from doing what *you* want.) Trust your friendship, and give your pal a little breathing room to meet other friends. Be confident in your friendship—things will be easier on everyone that way.

If she's a true friend, you're not going to lose her just because somebody new comes onto the scene. Her liking someone else has nothing to do with how much she cares about you. So appreciate your best bud. At the same time, don't be afraid to do a little friendship exploring yourself. You might find someone who makes you laugh at the stupidest stuff, or who knows a girl who knows the boy from a neighboring school that you've been crushing on!

After all, depending entirely on one friend for your social life can leave you feeling lonely and isolated. What happens when she goes on a family vacation, gets sick, doesn't want to do what you want to do, or just isn't around on a Friday night? We're not saying you need to hook yourself up with a "back-up" bud, but having options is nice.

The Friendship Triangle

If two's company...does three have to be a crowd?

You and Ashley have been two peas in a pod since you waddled around in diapers. You've had plenty of friends, but none that compare! But during second semester this year, Megan arrived and things have changed. Almost instantly you and Ashley agreed Megan was way cool. You have classes together, and Megan lives just doors down from you both—it's been awesome! But as summer approaches, things are starting to feel, well, weird. Is your triangle destined for disaster or is there room in that pod for one more?

Take this quiz to see if you're friendship triangle material. Do you wish things were like the old days—just you and Ash? Is Megan more your style? Or...are you ready to wave buh-bye to your duo and say hello to your trio? Find out!

1 **School's almost out (yippee!) and everyone's frantically penning poems and scribbling signatures in each other's yearbooks. You:**

a: reserve a full page for Ashley and the next page for Megan. You're psyched to have two totally special pages from your two best buds!

b: sign Ashley's yearbook, but don't fill the entire page because you leave out all that super-sappy, best friends forever stuff. Hey, things change, even best friends.

c: save Ashley a full page—it's tradition! Tell Megan she's welcome to sign any page you've reserved for "other friends."

2 It's time to plan your family's annual trip to the shore. As usual, you're allowed to invite a friend. What do you do?

a: Invite Megan. Ashley's come with you the last three years. And sometimes with Ashley it's the same old, same old. Megan's got the best stories, so you know you'll never be bored.

b: Invite Ashley, of course. She gets along so well with your family and you two are beach buds, always!

c: Beg your parents to let you invite both girls. If they say no, settle on having Ashley and Megan sleep over the entire weekend before your trip and resolve to spend beach week hanging with just the fam—you wouldn't want to look like you were picking favorites!

3 You three are spending the day at the nearby amusement park. You've been dying to duel the Monster, a lightning-fast, upside-down doozey of a coaster. Ashley is way too freaked to even look at it, so:

a: you and Megan go once. Ashley's off the hook for the first time ever and gladly opts for a cotton-candy break.

b: you plead with her to try it, even though you know she'll never budge. When Megan offers to go with you, you tell her you'd never ditch Ashley like that, and you'll go another time.

c: you and Megan spend the rest of the afternoon conquering the Monster. Since Ashley's a ride-wimp, you're pumped to have a partner who partakes. Ashley's a souvenir-shopper anyway. She'll be fine.

4 You all duck into one of those little photo booths for some wacky pics. After the first flash, you're all falling off the stool and crushing each other, so:

a: you suggest that Ashley sit out the next couple since you already have oodles of pictures together.

b: you tell Megan she's killing your leg and ask her to wait outside the booth.

c: you all grin and bear it! If you're not crowded and falling all over the place what's the point? That's what makes those little pics such keepers!

5 You invite Megan and Ashley over for a mini pool party and BBQ. But Megan calls that morning with a bad case of a stomach bug. Now what?

a: Ask your mom to break the bad news to Ashley when she arrives. Rush over to Megan's with some Pepto and DVDs!

b: Give Ashley a call and plan to get together ASAP to make Megan a slew of get-well cards and whip up a batch of instant-cheer peanut butter brownies for when she's feeling better.

c: Let Ashley know that Megan had to bail and suggest she come over earlier so you two can choreograph your annual synchronized swimming show!

6 **You and Ashley adore Lil' Bow Wow, and everyone knows it! Just last night you were squabbling over whose name sounds better with "Wow." When Megan disses him, you:**

a: agree that he's pretty much overrated and join her drool-fest over Freddie Prinze, Jr.

b: exchange expressions of sheer shock with Ashley. How dare she insult your little Wow!

c: have to laugh. Megan has a point—Freddie Prinze is way hot. But you and Ashley can't help loving Lil' Bow Wow. Once Megan sees his newest video for the fifteenth time, she'll agree!

7 **You and Ashley get into a disagreement. You:**

a: call Megan and give her the dish on how Ashley can be soooo mean.

b: apologize profusely—one night without chatting to Ashley is more than enough!

c: and Ashley keep Megan out of it. After all, it's between the two of you and no one else.

8 **You and Ashley play softball every summer. Megan says she'd love to join, but she stinks at softball and is picking up tap dancing instead. So:**

a: you and Ashley convince her to try out and promise to get her in tip-top softball shape!

b: you trade in your cleats for taps and tell Ashley you'll cheer her on when you're not dancing.

c: you agree that Megan might be happier tapping because your league's pretty competitive. You make plans to practice your fast pitch with Ashley.

9 **Ashley and Megan spent Saturday at the mall while you were stuck baby-sitting. The next day, you:**

a: call Ashley for the scoop and invite her to go to the movies with you that night. You're having Ashley withdrawal!

b: have them both over to show off the new duds they dug up.

c: call Megan and make plans to go to the pool, without Ashley—you need a little break from her.

10 **By summer's end, your other friends are saying:**

a: Who would have thunk it? You and Megan are now inseparable.

b: No surprises here. You and Ashley are still inseparable.

c: Wow! The three of you are inseparable.

SCORING
Add up your points then read on!

1.	**a:** 3	**b:** 2	**c:** 1	6.	**a:** 2	**b:** 1	**c:** 3
2.	**a:** 2	**b:** 1	**c:** 3	7.	**a:** 2	**b:** 1	**c:** 3
3.	**a:** 3	**b:** 1	**c:** 2	8.	**a:** 3	**b:** 2	**c:** 1
4.	**a:** 2	**b:** 1	**c:** 3	9.	**a:** 1	**b:** 3	**c:** 2
5.	**a:** 2	**b:** 3	**c:** 1	10.	**a:** 2	**b:** 1	**c:** 3

10-16 points: Make New Friends but Keep the Old!

You're no square, but given the choice, you'd mold that too-close-for-comfort triangle back into a circle, of two. Seems you've got the whole "keep the old" friends part, but you spaced on the "make new friends" part. You're not averse to making new friends, or even to sharing your BFF, but you're much happier one-on-one with a single best friend.

Though it's great you have what you need in one friend, make sure you're not prematurely pushing away a potentially fab friend. If all three of you hit it off, put out the extra effort to make things run smoothly. This doesn't mean things between you and your BFF have to change. There's nothing wrong with making plans to hang one-on-one with your old-time bud. If your new friend's worthy of your friendship, she should be cool with it. Just do your best to make sure nobody steps on anybody's toes—like ease up on all the inside jokes when you're with your new bud—save 'em for that annual beach trip with your BFF.

17-23 points: Out with the Old and in with the New

You and your BFF have always been buds, for sure! You value your friendship and the past you share, but sometimes a girl needs a change. Change can be scary and unsettling, but it can also be good. Change doesn't have to be drastic. If you're mega-clicking with a third, good for you! Don't hold back on meeting new buds because you feel guilty or disloyal to your BFF. You're allowed to make new friends, you're allowed to be excited about it and you're allowed to make plans with just your new bud. But, you're not allowed to make your true-blue feel like an outsider! And, if you've been super-tight for super-long it's easy to see how one of you might feel pushed aside when a new girl enters the scene. Resist the temptation to go all-out befriending someone else—your long-time friend is sure to feel slighted. Do your best to include your BFF when getting to know your new friend, and work together to become a true-blue trio. Nothing is worth risking a life-long friendship.

24-30 points: The Pinnacle of the Friendship Triangle

Good for you! Your healthy friendship with your best friend has made it easy for the two of you to welcome a new pal. Sounds like you've successfully side-stepped the third wheel pitfall. Nobody wants to feel like an outsider or an invader. And nobody wants to feel like they've been passed over for anyone else. Nice work! And you've clearly taken steps to make sure nobody feels like that.

Congratulations for taking care of each other's feelings and for including another friend into your circle—someone with whom you can share secrets, hang out, and have fun. Just because everything between your trio is hunky-dory, it doesn't mean you have to spend all your time together as a threesome. Pairing up for certain activities is perfectly fine, and there are some "friendship traditions" with your best friend that you'll want to keep just between the two of you. You've realized that a new friend can add to your friendship, not take away from it.

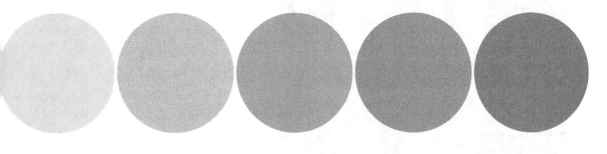

Tips for Turning a Twosome into a Threesome

Trust your friendship.
If you and your BFF have a solid friendship, nothing will weaken it. Even though you may feel occasional insecurity, realize that a new friend can add to the union.

Give each other breathing room.
If one of you wants to hang out with someone else occasionally, don't sweat it. It doesn't mean that your friendship is coming to an end.

It's okay to be jealous.
It's natural for you (or your BFF) to feel jealous when a third girl enters your life. Allow yourself to feel all kinds of emotions, but remember: Just because your BFF is hanging out with someone new, it doesn't mean you're toast.

Do things together as a trio.
Problems can arise when one side of the triangle feels left out. The trick is to make sure that all three of you feel secure, and one way is by doing things that three people can enjoy. Your new motto? The more, the merrier. Just remember this doesn't have to be a 24/7 thing—give each other breathing room.

Explore other friendships.
If your BFF is keeping busy with someone else, get out there and meet other girls. Who knows? You could even turn your twosome into a fabulous foursome!

HELP! What to Do When...

Chapter 5

FriendShip DiLemmas and HOW to HandLe Them

Every friendship has those tricky, sticky situations that pop up when you least expect (or want!) them. Here's how to handle the little things that make you go grrr—before they become big things!

What to do when...

...she has a not-so-nice habit of getting a laugh at your expense.

She's so funny you forgot to laugh? One thing worse than a friend who always has to be in the spotlight is a friend who puts you down to get there. Like when she gave the soccer team a play-by-play of the time your puppy dragged your undies into the dining room during dinner. Everybody got a good laugh...but at your expense. Find out here if your friend even knows that she's always making you the butt of her jokes—and making you want to kick hers.

The Facts of Life

Stupid, embarrassing stuff happens to everyone. But some stupid, embarrassing stuff is *private*. When those very personal moments are repeated for public consumption, feelings get hurt. It's OK for a friend to laugh when you were hilariously gassy during your Saturday-night sleepover. But when she tells your crush all about it on Monday morning, that's just downright uncool. Friends should let friends relay their own funny anecdotes. That way, they're laughing *with* you, not *at* you. See the difference?

Sit Down, Ms. Stand Up

If your bud's constant comedic routine is making you blue, say something. She probably doesn't even realize her offhand remarks are offensive to you. Tell her you appreciate her sense of humor, but her jokes need to be directed *away* from you. She's close to you, so she has a lot to say on the subject of you, and that's cool. But when it's unflattering, or when she reveals things that should stay between you, it's breaking your BFF bond. Hopefully, she'll get it.

Ha, Ha, HUH?

What to do if your friend is a creature of habit and launches into a "listen to this one"? Don't tell her to stick a cork in it, and don't storm off.

Also, don't try topping her whopper by blasting her back. You don't want to get into an all-out who-can-humiliate-whom-more war. Try a little subtlety. Give her a "look" only a best friend would understand. If that fails, discreetly say, "Please, don't go there." Feeling brave? Cut her off at the gate, and tell the story yourself. Any girl who can laugh at herself has got to be cool.

What's My Line?

You've told her to chill, but Miss Funny Gal continues to humiliate you? Pull her aside and ask her to agree to a secret code ("Yadda Yadda") or a signal (a scratch of the nose) that says, "Bud, you're stepping on my toes." If she keeps at it, it could be time to reevaluate the friendship. No joke!

She's your bestest bud. But there's this one little thing she does that makes your neck hair stand up as if to scream "HELLO!" Here's how to handle a pesky peeve without getting cranky at your girl friend:

Figure Out Exactly What's Bugging You

Can you describe your friend's bothersome behavior in six words or less? Like this: "She always fishes for compliments." If your answer sounds vague, like, "I don't know—she just drives me crazy," you need to get specific. Are *you* just irritable and taking it out on your friend? Or did she do something to really upset you? Figure it out.

Let the Little Stuff Go

When you spend 24/7 with a bud, there are bound to be things that bug you. But that doesn't mean friends should necessarily change—or can. Your bud snores at sleepovers? Can't carry a tune? There's nothing she can do about those irritating things, so it's up to you to adore her in spite of them. (And invest in a good pair of earplugs!)

When It's Not So Small

There are things a person actually does have control over. If your friend is flirting with your brother or punching you in a joking way (that hurts!), speak up. If something genuinely irritates you and she can stop it, tell her. Unless she's psychic, she can't read your mind. And tell her, don't attack her, like this: "I don't want to nag you, but when you smack your gum during a movie, I can't hear a thing." Don't go on and on about it. Just say it. And don't be surprised if her feelings are hurt. Nobody likes to be told she's annoying. So give her a chance to absorb what you've said, and continue to treat her like the best bud she is.

Pals stick together, help out in a pinch, and keep promises. Right? If your bud has a bad habit of ditching out on plans, here's how to cope with her flakiness.

The Set-up

Ashley, Sarah, and Katie are planning a Valentine's Day party at Katie's house. They're all pitching in to pull this party off superbly. Since Ashley is notorious for last-minute bailing, the other girls make her double-swear she won't skip on the party prepping. They agree to meet at noon the next day to start decorating and making the chow.

The Ditch

At 11 a.m. the following day, Ashley calls to say she totally spaced on previous plans to shop with her mom. She's available late afternoon, though. Sarah and Katie decide not to wait. They have endless batches of heart-shaped cookies to make, not to mention all those red and pink balloons to blow up. That afternoon, Ashley posts just in time to sample a cookie and hang up one last streamer. And, even though she barely put forth a fraction of the effort, Ashley gets to have 100-percent of the fun! Aaaargh! Experiencing anything similar with a friend?

The Response

Here's what you should remember when a friend lets you down: If it's a first-time flake-out or she has a legit excuse, don't make a stink. But if she has an excuse rap sheet longer than your guest list, you have a right to be bummed. And you need to say something to her about it because she might not have a clue she upset you. Say nothing, and it will likely happen again.

If she's just flighty and forgetful by nature, learn to accept your friend for the way she is. And that means not setting yourself up for a fall. You know she's not dependable, so don't expect her to commit to stuff. Is she always late? Tell her little fibs about when you need her somewhere so she can arrive on time, even though she'll still think she's late. You don't have to ditch a fun friend just because she's flighty. But when you need a friend you can count on, include somebody else, OK?

...she acts like a total diva!

All the world's a stage...but is your best friend always the star of the show? When drama queens are just goofing around, their theatrics can be downright funny. But sometimes the drama can turn into unnecessary *melodrama*. Does she act like the sky is falling if she gets a B on a quiz? Does she totally freak when her crush chats with another girl? *Girls' Life* readers share tips for taming "The Diva."

Attention, Attention!

Maybe she's aching for attention. Or maybe she's really hyper, and it's just her personality. Grace, 10, says, "My best friend can be so annoying! She thinks she has to add little lies and exaggerations to every story. And she's in every school performance and always gets the lead. This just adds fuel to the fire."

Laura, 10, also gets fed up with her friend's attention-seeking: "My BFF goes into spin-cycle when anyone disagrees with her. And any kind of stress, like a big test, can make her switch into overdrive. Sometimes I just have to tune her out."

Enough Encores!

Tuning your friend out can work wonders, but then what about the times when she really needs you to hear her? Or she's saying something that you need to hear? You can't ignore your best friend all the time just because she's often overly dramatic—that's her! And you have to love her for who she is. But that doesn't mean you can't learn to manage your Diva.

Suggestions for quelling the queen? "She's just that way, so I listen for a while," says Kelly, 10. "Then if it's out of control, like she's getting loud or going on too long, I'll slowly hold up my finger to my lips, smile and go 'Shhhhhhh!' at her. She knows she gets carried away, and that's our cue for when she needs to slow down with the drama."

Kaley, 11, handles the outbursts differently: "I just remind myself that even though my BFF exaggerates, she tells a good story. Whenever she goes overboard, I just play along or start laughing. Sometimes I'll keep her in check by saying stuff like, 'How big was the fish? How long did you hold your breath?' And she giggles and gives me the real detail. It's like a game between us now. I love her outbursts!"

The Award Goes To...

She's exciting. She's funny. And she drives you bananas. But, she's your best friend! Ariel, 11, says, "She's a major diva! Everything is a big deal! But I love her for who she is inside, and that's why she's my BFF—despite the repeat performances over grades and crush woes." Appreciate her need for attention and her humor. Come up with ways to tame her, like Kelly's cue to shush her friend. But if you need an intermission, by all means take one before you toss her off the stage!

...she makes summer plans that don't include you!

Did you say your best friend is going away for the summer? Oh dear. How could she leave you flying solo when she's your full-rotation hang buddy? You want to be happy that she gets to go to a cool camp or spend time at her aunt's beach condo, but the truth is, now it feels like it's going to be one bummer of a summer. But it doesn't have to be. Here's how to see the sunny side....

Don't Hold It Against Her

It's understandable that you're disappointed, but that's no reason to sulk or stomp all over your friend's plans. She's not trying to hurt you or abandon you. In fact, maybe her folks are forcing her to stay on the farm with her cousins. But if she's totally stoked, be a true-blue bud and tell her to have a good time. If things were reversed, you'd want the same sweet send-off.

Make Your Own Plans

You don't want to squander the summer feeling sorry for yourself, so it's time to map out fun plans to stay busy. For inspiration, check out books on summer adventure programs. Or hop on the Web to find out what programs your local rec center or YMCA offers. Maybe you could even land a regular babysitting gig and save money for some cool back-to-school clothes. And volunteering at the library isn't such a bad idea either. Hey, it's air-conditioned!

Befriend a Few New Buds

Finding new summer friends is not finding replacements for your best friend or an attempt to make her jealous. It's a good thing to find new gal pals to hang with anyway, but if you're homebound without your best bud all summer, it's ideal. Think of it as social insurance for a summer of fun, best friend around or not!

Stay in Touch

OK, so your girl is far away for the summer. You can still correspond with her whenever you want, right? Hopefully, you can e-mail and have IM chats. If online talking isn't an option, why not give her a long-distance calling card as a going-away present? If

76

she's off to a rural camp, get the P.O. box address so you can write letters back and forth. Easy!

Don't Freak If You Don't Hear From Her

She hasn't forgotten you. She's probably keeping busy to cure any homesickness, or she's caught up in her new experience. When you go on a trip or move somewhere for a season, sometimes it's easier to remain anonymous, and wait until you return to get back into your regular life. She's doing her thing. Do yours. You two will get it together when she's back, and it'll probably soon feel like she never even left!

...she kinda fades away in the summer!

Before you get too stoked about long, lazy tankini days, consider that summer break could come at a cost—to your friendship. During school, hanging out is automatic. But despite summer's freedom, it's plagued with potential separation pitfalls—especially if you and your buds don't live a hop, skip, and a jump away.

But don't throw in the beach towel just yet. Plan ahead to hook up, being sure to run it past the 'rents before marking your calendar. Busy parents hate getting word of plans 15 minutes before you need a lift. Springing stuff like that on Mom might make her a much less willing chauffeur.

Make Things as Simple as Possible for Everyone

Can Mom drop you at your BFF's for the day on her way to work? Maybe both moms could meet halfway. If the mall's a midpoint, why not meet there? An older sis has wheels? Hit her up for a ride. If you have a third friend you want to hang with, see if her parents can shuffle you all around.

For More Frequent Fun, Sign Up for a Week of Soccer Camp Together

Or volunteer as rec counselors at a local day camp for kiddies. Grace, 12, always makes it a point to throw a huge mid-summer bash. "I invite every girl I know, and we swim, pig-out and catch up. It's awesome! And when we get back to school, it's not so weird."

If It's Been Awhile, Don't Assume She Doesn't Want to Chat

Pick up the phone, and give her a ring. Catch up on stuff, and tell her you miss her. You'll likely wonder why you didn't call earlier. With a little bit of effort, you'll send summer separation anxiety packing!

You spent the summer in one place and your best friend spent the summer somewhere else. You missed her being so far away, but then when you finally hook up at summer's end, it seems you're farther apart than ever. Are things really different? Ally, 12, shares: "My BFF volunteered at an environmental organization and met girls who shared her passion for saving trees from deforestation. I was psyched for her, but all she wanted to talk about was how much she bonded with them. We'd been friends for five years, but it seemed like she couldn't relate to me."

How does a friendship survive the inevitable changes in friends' lives? Here are some ideas for making sure your friendship reunions are right where you want them to be.

Give It Time

Even though you want to wave a wand to make the old vibe come back, it's important to give your-selves time to get back in the swing of things. You both need to come off the summer experience and find your 'home' selves again. It might take a few weeks, so be patient. "When Marne came back from horse camp, I couldn't stand all her bragging about riding in the hills all day and how lucky she was to get away from the city," says Brenda, 11. "But after a few weeks, she just quit talking about camp, and her horse obsession stopped. We were right back to our old routine."

Dig Her New Self

You've given it a couple of weeks and things still don't feel as warm and right as they used to. She's had her summer, her experiences without you, and she's like a whole other person. It's her, but she's different. But consider that she may be thinking the exact same thing about you. Instead of trying to get "back" your old friend, why not get acquainted with the new one? And she can do the same with you. You might like what you find better.

Says Lori, 10: "My friend's grandma died over the summer, so she spent a month with her mom helping her grandpa. When she came back, she was so sad and serious. At first I thought she was a big bummer. But then I saw she became a much more sensitive friend. Now we really talk about important things, not just what we want to do on Friday night."

You're back at school and can't wait to hang with your friends. But hold up! Since when has everyone become so cliquey? Do they know they're being awful? Cut the catty clique cord here.

Too Cool for School

Whitney, 11, says some of her friends "exclude others at lunch and on the bus. They think they're just being choosey about their friends, but really they're judging people and bad-vibing everyone with their 'only our clique' energy." Whitney kept these girls as friends, but also hangs out with other girls.

A Voice From the Other Side

Cliques have power because there is safety in numbers. But what if the clique's power sucks you in? Amy, 11, admits this: "I joined in on my friends' nastiness. I was like, 'Oh, yuck, check out her outfit! Where does she shop? Tacky.com?' One day I realized we were all criticizing each other, too. We totally talked trash on whoever wasn't in the room. I started feeling really bad about myself." When Amy stopped joining in on the dissing, her group ditched her. Even though it will take some time for her to shake her Cruella rep, she's happier now. "I don't need to put people down to feel better about myself," she says. "And my new friends are so cool and supportive and never tease people for being themselves."

Silence the Snobs

Is your group a bunch of meanies? Do you guys say negative stuff about other people? Do you talk about your own friends if they're not within earshot? Sometimes, in the cocoon of a group, we don't realize we're totally going off on people and saying unflattering things out of a weird momentum of gossip. But we shouldn't. Putting people down, excluding people, dismissing people, and basically acting superior isn't cool at all. If your friends treat people in this crummy way, see if you can show them the light. If they treat you this way, show yourself the door. Good people don't let themselves get treated badly or treat others badly. Clique or no clique, you shouldn't be watching your back—you should be spreading your wings. For real, you deserve friends who will help you fly.

He's not your boyfriend. He's your boy...friend. Excellent!

Why a Boy?

With boys, friendship is a totally different ball game, or so it seems. But then there are those boys who don't fit the typical boy mold. They don't have Nintendo Thumb, they don't act like they hate you, they actually seem interested in things other than skateboards and sports. It's these boys that make great friends.

"Our friendship started because I had a crush on him," says Krissy, 13. "But, after hanging out, I realized I didn't want to go out with him, just *hang* out with him. We had a bunch of classes together, so we talked a lot during the day. Then we started studying together. Now we're best friends." Give a boy a chance to be your friend, and you might find a new, understanding, and totally trustworthy bud.

The Best Part

"It's great having a boy BFF," says Chris, 11. "I learn how boys think and get the dirt on my crushes." Sandra, 14, says this: "I don't like him—I love him! He's always there for me and ready to talk about everything from girl stuff, like friendship jealousies, to my new cheerleading moves." Many readers say their boy friends are easier to talk to and better at keeping secrets than some girl friends.

Plus, Laura, 12, says, "It's great hanging with my boy BFF because he loves to do different kinds of stuff. My girl friends sit around listening to CDs and talking. Rich and I always get out and do things. He's always up for mini-golf, shooting hoops or just going for an afternoon hike."

Boys can also be great for giving you a different opinion on things than your gal BFFs. "When I ask my friend Amelia for advice, she goes on and on and gives me about ten different options of what to do and sometimes that's not really helpful," says Alicia, 11. "But my friend Brian will listen, think about it for a few minutes and then just tell me what he'd do in the situation. No wishy-washy answers. I think boys are better at getting to the point."

The Weird Part

What if you start to crush on your boy friend? If you think it's mutual, you could try telling him. If you don't think it's mutual, zipping your lips is your best plan. If he tells you he's crushing on you (and you're not on him), it's time to talk it through. True friends can clear any hurdle.

Another common problem with boy friends is jealousy from other girls. Trouble may start if a girl friend of yours crushes on your bud. Or worse, your boy gets a new girlfriend who doesn't like him having a girl for a friend.

Says Meg, 13, "Ryan and I had been best friends for years, until he started dating Shannon. Then he didn't have time for me any more. I finally said something to him, and now we try to hang out once a week."

So how do you become "just friends" with a boy? Granted going up to a random boy and inviting him to join you for a tennis match on Saturday might give him the wrong idea, so it's best to start slow and strengthen your friendships with the great boys you already know.

Many girls shy away from boy friendships for fear of things getting weird, so you should go out of your way to send a sweet but strictly friend vibe. Treat him with the same interest and respect you would any friend. Who knows? You might find a great new BFF (that's *boy* friend forever!).

This guy and I have been friends since kindergarten. He has a new GF, and she invades our space. He's also been acting different. I'm afraid of losing him. What should I do?

Chances are he has no clue you feel neglected—boys can be oblivious about this stuff. So, tell him you miss him and, for whatever reason, you feel he's acting different. Acknowledge that you want him to be happy and that you're glad he has a girlfriend. Tell him you value the friendship and would love it if you two could spend some solo time together like you used to. But also say it would be cool to hang with him and his girl sometimes— that way, he shouldn't be uncomfortable inviting you to tag along once in a while. Be nice to him and his GF. If you're friendly toward her (and not too friendly with him), they should be OK with you. Whatever you do, don't end the friendship because you'll probably be around longer than she will—but keep that one to yourself! If you're sincere, he should make adjustments to fit you into his schedule.

When dollars and cents are added to the friendship equation, things can get tricky. Girls on both sides of the issue may experience similar emotions—discomfort, jealousy and embarrassment—but for different reasons. One bud has a lot of dough, the other has very little. Here's how to make sure money doesn't make you lose your common sense about your friendship.

Red in the Face

When you hit the mall, you bring your hard-earned babysitting bucks. She grabs Dad's plastic and votes to hit the Guess store. Sounds good, if all you want to buy are some cute socks! Obviously, being short on cash can be disappointing, and sometimes even embarrassing.

But being on the flip side of the coin can be hard, too. Katie, 11, says, "I shop in department stores and boutiques, and my BFF shops discount. So when we go to the mall, I feel weird. She'll say, 'You're crazy! Why are you spending $70 when you can get practically the same pants for $20 at Wal-Mart?'"

Green with Envy

Ronnie, 10, says, "My best friend has much more moolah than I do. She lives in a mansion, has super nice cars, and a secret passage from her bedroom into a private TV room! She's fun, but sometimes I feel strange, something I don't feel when I'm with my other friends. Sometimes I wish I had her life."

It's natural to be envious when your friend seems to have it all. Even if she's cool about her cash flow, you might get a wee bit jealous. Ever consider the grass might be green on both sides of the fence? Your rich bud might envy you! Just because she has new clothes out the wazoo, doesn't mean her life is cake. Everyone has problems, things to deal with, issues to work out. Your friend has plenty of material things, but if you look past her designer outfits, you'll find she's not so different from you.

Be True-blue

A LOL humor break can take the edge off a tense money moment. If you're feeling like Spam compared to your friend's filet mignon, don't. So what if your whole house could fit into her kitchen? Hey, the cash belongs to her parents anyway. It's not her money, after all. She just lives there! So don't be intimidated by your well-to-do friend. The bucks don't make the bud. Says Katie, "Sometimes, I feel bad that my BFF can't afford things I can.

Life isn't fair when it comes to money. We should be grateful for what we have—family, friends, health. What's money if you don't have those things?" Right on, Katie!

Your best friend is your friend for reasons that have nothing to do with money. It can get in the way sometimes, but remember that it's just a movie, a trip to the mall, a moment involving cash that's of no real value to how you feel about your friend.

...you and your BFF have WAY different bods!

You and your best friend couldn't be more different body-wise. She's got a great figure, and you, well, you're still growing! Or maybe it's that she's super lean and you haven't lost your baby fat yet? Different body types—especially if your best friend is developing faster than you—can trigger some sizable insecurities. Here's how your friendship can still measure up, even when one of you measures far more or far less than the other.

Trigger One:
Shop Then Drop

When you're totally different heights, sizes, or both, shopping can be great (you'll never buy the same things!) or it can be awful (she looks good in everything, and you're sure there's a conspiracy against girls over a size 10). "I'm so much bigger than my

BFF," says Julia, 12, "I weigh at least 20 pounds more than she does, so lots of trends look ridiculous on me. When we go shopping, I have a terrible time finding stuff that flatters me, but she looks great in everything she tries on. It makes me feel so ugly."

Bigger Size Wise

Says Lisa, 11, "When my best friend and I go to the mall, she heads right for the kids' department while I go off to juniors—she's just too little to fit into anything above a girls' size 12. But my friend doesn't care at all, and she's always bragging about how much cheaper the girls' department is. Her attitude is awesome."

If your friend is a lean body type and you're not, shopping can be a test of your self-esteem. But it doesn't help anyone for you to judge your inside by your friend's outside. She's skinny. So what? Keep living your life! Try on clothes you like—threads that work with your body type. Shopping isn't a contest of who fits into what or who tries on more clothes.

Smaller Size Wise

When Fern, 12, and her best friend go shopping, things can get weird: "Once, we wanted the same pair of jeans, and the salesperson goes, 'This size is great for you.' Then she looked at my friend and said, 'But you need a bigger pair, my dear.' It made us both uncomfortable. Now, she avoids shopping with me!"

If shopping is this stressful, address it. You love your friend just the way she is, so tell her! Maybe you're even a little envious of her curves. But if going into stores that carry smaller sizes truly makes her squirm, don't beg or make her go in. And don't forget there are plenty of stores that stock stuff for girls of any size.

And, please, don't rub your pint-size physique in her face ("Oh, these pants are falling off my waist!"). And finally, it's OK to secretly love that you score major deals off the kiddie clearance rack!

Trigger Two: Closet Case

Lots of girls don't even need to hit the mall to feel dress stress—it can come out with the mere mention of clothes. A girl who's insecure about her body (and envious of her friend's figure) might tease or make snide remarks about her friend's new mini. "I don't know why I said it," says Felicia, 11, "but my friend was wearing these super low-rise jeans, and they looked good, but I said 'You're so skinny that you look like a torso on two Popsicle sticks.' My friend was suddenly worried that she looked dumb—she looked amazing!—and didn't wear her hot new jeans to the dance. I felt so bad." Is it obvious to you that Felicia was just a little jealous? Should be.

Bigger Size Wise

"I'm in eighth grade and I have six best friends, and all of them are smaller than I am," says Lauren, 13. "None of them seem to notice, but I do. I am the only one who can't share clothes. I feel big and oafy."

Says Emily, 12, "The cool part about being bigger than my buds is that I don't ever have to lend my stuff out and worry about it getting messed up. But I do feel left out when I can't be part of a clothes swap."

Try this: Instead of thinking of yourself as bigger, why not think of yourself as just different? Being unique is delicious! And there's nothing more attractive than an air of self-confidence. Love your height, your hips, or whatever! Develop your own look, and be confident. Just because you're friends, doesn't mean you all have to look alike and dress alike—how dull! Next time the girls get together to share clothes, suggest swapping accessories too—scarves, jewelry and hair things are one-size-fits-all. Just because you're not a petite size doesn't mean you have to wear baggy clothes!

Smaller Size Wise

Paige, 12, says, "My friend weighs at least 40 pounds more than I do, but she's also six inches taller. She gets jealous, but she doesn't know I get jealous of her, too. More cool clothes fit her. I can only buy kids' clothes."

The thing about friends is, you like a lot of the same stuff. It's one of the reasons you're friends to begin with. Haven't you ever spent hours getting ready to go out, only to meet up with your friends and discover you all look like some version of Destiny's Child? There are only so many trends out there. The bonus to being small with a bigger friend is the avoidance of "friend cloning." Even though you could be wearing the same style, it's going to look much different on different body types

Amanda, 11, says this: "When my best friend, Jane, and I were in grammar school, we were identical. We could show up at school wearing exactly the same clothes, and boys would tease us, saying that we called each other the night before. We both have brown hair and hazel eyes. But then she grew to 5' 6" by the seventh grade, and I'm only 4' 11"! We like to joke that we share the same brain, so it's sort of a relief not to look like her anymore."

So you're shorter, or smaller. So she's one body and you're another. Who cares! It's what's inside, right? If you let your outsides get in the way of your friendship, then that's just silly. Love your body, how it's changing, what it looks like, how it feels. That's all you need to think about when it comes to yourself, your best friends, and your body types. Honest.

Is your best bud moving? It happens. Just when you're sure your life is fine and dandy, something or someone pulls the comfy rug from underneath your feet. It's sad that your friend is leaving, but the truth is she's relocating, not dying! She'll still be your friend, just not so full time. Here are some tips on dealing with how to keep your friendship close after your bud moves away.

Getting the News

When your BFF tells you the sad news about her move, it's best not to start mourning right away. She's probably feeling as bad as you are.

Be supportive and try to make the most of it. Spend time together having fun, not crying over the inevitable move. "I made my BFF all her favorite food one night, and then we did a mini photo shoot so we would have new pictures to put in our rooms," says Gina, 13. "It was sad when she left, but I felt like I sent her off in a good way."

The Big Day

The moving trucks are loaded, and you and your friend are sitting on her porch. You haven't said much—you want your good-bye to be short, sweet, and sincere. Finding the right words can be the hardest part. There are no perfect words, only sincere ones. But, hey, she'll still be your friend, just from afar! And you'll always have e-mail and can call each other.

The New School Year...Without Her

You meet your friends at the normal spot to catch up on gossip, check out the first-day clothes, see who got which teacher. But it's not as cool as it usually is. Your other friends seem to have a best friend to be with, but not you. It's obvious what's missing here. SHE is.

Where to begin? Start by being the first person to say "hi" to any new kids at your school. There is always a girl who is new to school, just like your friend will be new to hers. Ask her where she's from, and see if she wants to join you and your friends at lunch. She'll surely be grateful, and you've got a potential new friend to get to know. Just make sure every other word out of your mouth is not about how great your old best friend is!

Make New Friends and Keep the Old

After the shock of your friend's exit subsides, things start to get back to normal. No one can blame you for feeling blue and missing your chum. But after a couple days or a couple weeks, whatever you need, you will start to feel like the world isn't so empty without her. You'll be back on your feet, hanging with other friends, maybe even bonding with a new BFF. Now is the time to realize you have the best of both worlds. IM with your friend so you get her humor, love, wisdom, and support. Or start a tradition of writing a snail-mail letter to each other once a week.

Says Jackie, 12: "I was so sad when Alex left. But then I started writing letters to her, and she would write me, and pretty soon I was so into the letters, I forgot I was sad! I started meeting other kids, and I got to know this one girl I had in math last year, and it was so cool. In a way, good things came out of Alex's leaving because I feel closer than ever to her, and I also have a new friend."

HELP!

I'm moving to Hawaii. I'm really excited about living near the beach, but I don't want to leave my friends. My dad is in the military, so I've done this before —but it's different this time because I've made such special friends. How can I keep my old friendships back at home and make some cool new friends in Hawaii?

Having to move away from your good friends totally stinks. But think of your upcoming move as a great opportunity to meet some new buds. Stay in touch with your true-blues via e-mail and calls. We're not going to say it'll be easy, because it won't be. It's tough when you're not there for all the day-to-day stuff. On the other hand, friends should be psyched to talk to someone who can be objective and caring. Plus, think of all the cool Hawaii stories you'll be able to share. As for making new pals on the Big Island, show interest in your new classmates and neighbors. Take up an after-school sport, join chorus or volunteer with your local youth group. Get involved with things you like, and you're bound to meet a bunch of great new friends!

Quiz

Are You a Gossip-friendly Gal Pal?

What would you do if your BFF became the target of gossip gone wild? Are you the kind of gal who's never met a juicy tidbit she didn't want to get her mitts on and toss around? Or would you swear up and down to protect a friend—even if it meant stretching the truth? Not sure what you'd do? Take this quiz to find out if you're a sideliner, heavy hitter, or team-player when it comes to fielding gossip that's going around about your BFF.

1 **Word is your BFF spent Saturday night with her crush. Your BFF denies it and is telling everyone she was with you—but she wasn't! What do you do?**

a: Swear on your cat's life she was with you.

b: Go along with it this time... but only because it's a rush to be in the midst of the mayhem! No denying it— this is good gossip!

c: You have no clue what went on that night, but she can forget it if she thinks you're going down with her. When asked, you shrug your shoulders and say, "I don't know what's going on. I spent the week-end at my dad's," because you did.

2 **A pal slipped that your mutual friend's fam might be having financial problems. Your BFF hasn't said a word to you, but she'd freak if she knew people were gossiping about her family's private biz. What do you do?**

a: Give the gossipmongers a piece of your mind. When it comes to family matters, it's totally uncool to blab!

b: Investigate. Hmmm, you must get as much dirt as possible. This is major! Once you get the scoop, you'll hint to your friend that you know something...and then offer to spring for her lunch.

c: Yikes, this is serious. Before getting involved, you'd ask your parents for their worldly advice since you wouldn't want to do or say the wrong thing. They always point you in the right direction.

3 In the locker room before b-ball practice, some girls are dissing your BFF's fashionista efforts for last Friday's dance. She spent weeks painstakingly perfecting her wraparound-lace/pinstripe ensemble, but these girls can't stop talking about her Salvation Army clown suit." What do you do?

a: Interrupt the jokesters with a nice, big locker slam. "Um, hello? Who are you—the fashion police? Here's a thought: Instead of focusing on someone else's business, think you could focus on actually getting the ball in the basket today?"

b: Play it cool. Those girls are always on the inside loop. No need to ruin your link to Grand Gossip Central. Besides, "Salvation Army clown suit" *is* pretty funny.

c: You're tempted to shout, "So what if she wasn't dressed in head-to-toe GAP like you clones!?" But why cause a scene? When practice lets out, you'll kindly tell your BFF what they said.

4 Your two best friends, Amanda and Ashley, are on the outs because Amanda has been spilling Ashley's secrets. Amanda has made a buddy boo-boo, but, if you get on her about it, your secrets could be next! What do you do?

a: You stick up for friends, no matter what, but Amanda's disloyalty upsets you and, worse, she really hurt Ashley. You can't ignore that. You'd remind Amanda that keeping secrets is crucial to friendships and to *please* not be so outspoken with *your* personal life, too.

b: You'd be a fool to take sides. It totally stinks that Amanda got busted blabbing, but her loose lips have brought some for-real excitement to your social life! Anyway, what are you— a referee?

c: Think Switzerland and stay neutral. You'd back off and let the two of them work it out. Why take sides? It'd just complicate things.

• •

If you got mostly A's, you're
The buddy-guard

As far as friends go, you're at the top of the list. You've got your bud's back, no matter what! So what if you have to stretch the truth a tad? The way you see it, there's only one way—the loyal way. Your friends trust you, and that's a cool thing. But there's a downside. What happens if she expects you to cover for her, like, *all* the time? Covering for her "crimes" could make you an unwitting accomplice. Even if you're clean as a whistle, you're guilty by association. Or, just as bad, a total doormat. Though people might respect your loyalty, they'll also see that you'd do anything to protect your friend—even lie to them. A BFF who'd put your reputation on the line is more concerned with saving her own neck. Keep things in perspective and, in the end, you might decide that sometimes loyalty has its limits!

The fearless entertainer

You're sociable and charming, and that's probably why gossip has no trouble making its way to your ears. You've got a direct line to the latest, greatest dirt. And, well, you've never had a problem passing along the scoop. Being an insider on what's what can definitely be exciting stuff. Your philosophy is this: If someone tells you something, it's fair game— even if it's not always a friendly game. You probably have plenty of pals who seek you out for details when major stuff goes down—but you might have trouble maintaining super-tight friendships. Has gossip ever gotten you into trouble? Has it ever destroyed a bud bond? If so, it's time to chill. People might like to share good, juicy gossip with you but, pretty soon, that's all you'll be— the goddess of gossip. It only takes a couple spills before girls will learn to think twice before telling you a darn

thing. Plus, the more gossip you dole out, the more likely it is that you'll be passing along false or exaggerated info. And the only thing people like less than a gossip is an unreliable one! It's OK to dig into some friendly gossip with your pals—just keep their secrets, well, secret!

The honest amiga

You're all about keeping it real. You're a fab friend, but twisting the truth just isn't your thing. Why risk your own stellar rep just to cover for someone else's gab-gone-mad? But is honesty always the best policy? Would you confirm one of your close pal's top secrets for the whole gang just because they asked? Sometimes, playing dumb or saying you're not at liberty to discuss something is better than blurting out the dirt. Maybe you've sensed that you're occasionally banished from the circle of all things gossipy. So what? Since you don't want to sell out your friends anyway, perhaps being less in the know isn't such a bad thing after all. If you *are* hanging with a group of friends who are gabbing about stuff that makes you uncomfy or sense that you're about to be put in a compromising position ("Is Brittany really crushing on Jason?"), your best bet could be to change the subject pronto or take a quick lap around the non-fiction section of the library. There truly *are* times when ignorance is bliss.

Friendship Problems

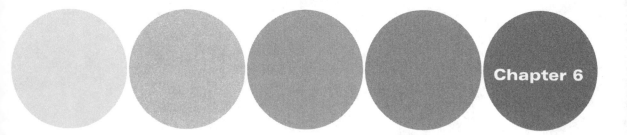

Chapter 6

Quiz

True Blue Bud or Farewell Friend?

You were friends, but...now? This quiz will help you figure out if you and your friend are in for smooth sailing or if your friendship has hit an iceberg.

1 After school, you can usually find your best bud...

a: hauling down to the gym to change for cheerleading, and then grabbing a snack before her violin lesson.

b: with the new girl, Amber, whispering about some boy.

c: where she always is— waiting by the fence for you.

2 Yikes! There's a rumor going around school that you cheated on the Spanish quiz. You can count on your friend to...

a: tell people, "No way, José!"

b: be sympathetic—when you finally track her down two days later.

c: adamantly deny that she's the one you copied off.

your HeLp!

My BFF gets so moody. How do I get her to stop taking things out on me that aren't my fault?

If you're tired of it, confront her nicely. Tell her it hurts your feelings. And listen to her point of view. Suggest to her that when she gets mad, she should talk it out with you instead of blaming you.

—Ashley T., 10

Say, "If you're in a bad mood, don't think you can take it out on me." Don't say it in a snobby voice because it may start a fight. If it continues, tell her you need a break from her but that you still want to be her friend.

—Liz, 9

I'd probably ask her why she is getting in these bad moods and if I could help her somehow. If that didn't work, I would have to tell her straight out, "I'm not causing your bad mood, so please stop blaming me for it."

—Ashley Z., 9

I would ask her to go ice skating with me or do something together we both enjoy so she could let out her anger. I would try to understand how she feels and listen to her. Above all, I would try not to take it personally.

—Ann, 11

When your friend chews you out, tell her to beat up a pillow or write in a journal. Suggest she join kickboxing, karate, or tae-bo. Sign up for classes with her. If she continues, tell her you care about her but not to scream at you.

—Sophie, 12

3 You've got mail! Your pal's e-mail is...

a: a lame excuse for blowing you off on the trip to the mall you two had planned.

b: a funny top-10 list she's group e-mailing to the gang.

c: all the great dish you missed that day.

4 This weekend, your friend's plans are...

a: going to softball practice, dashing home, reading a hundred pages of the *Grapes of Wrath* for Monday's book report, and babysitting for her sister. And that's just for Friday!

b: going around with her new friend Amber, looking for her crush.

c: seeing a movie at the mall (with you) and then pigging out on chili cheese fries (with you).

5 You just splurged on a cool new dress. Your bud...

a: tells you how awesome you look and offers to loan you her new feather bag to go with it.

b: wonders out loud if the wardrobe department from *That 70's Show* lent you the dress for the night.

c: tells you how great it looked on you at the holiday formal. Hello?

6 **Your friend just won four tickets to Aaron Carter. One for Mom, one for Dad and the extra one goes to...**

a: her cool cousin, Mandy. Family before friends.

b: her younger sis. Oh, well, you can't win 'em all.

c: you, right after she returns the Aaron Carter CD she borrowed from you four months ago.

7 **When you call, your friend...**

a: jumps right on the line and starts with her usual 15-minute monologue that always starts with, "You'll never guess what happened to me today!"

b: promises to call you back the second she gets done making her famous chicken pot pie— and she does.

c: tells her mom to say she's going to the library, but you guess she's probably heading over to hang out in the bleachers, and watch her beloved warm the bench during a baseball game.

8 **Your bud's got some juicy gossip, and you know she'll...**

a: give you the full scoop on the phone after she's done cramming for her science test.

b: sing like a canary the second the substitute teacher is done taking attendance.

c: make sure you're the last to know. After all, the story is about how hilarious it was when you snorted milk out your nose in front of your crush at lunch yesterday.

SCORING
Add up your total points then read on!

1.	**a:** 2	**b:** 3	**c:** 1	5.	**a:** 1	**b:** 3	**c:** 2
2.	**a:** 1	**b:** 3	**c:** 2	6.	**a:** 3	**b:** 2	**c:** 1
3.	**a:** 3	**b:** 2	**c:** 1	7.	**a:** 2	**b:** 1	**c:** 3
4.	**a:** 2	**b:** 3	**c:** 1	8.	**a:** 2	**b:** 1	**c:** 3

8-11 points: Smooth Sailing

Your friend is interested and involved. She realizes that to have you as a friend, she has to *be* a friend. That means taking an active part in keeping the lines of communication open and your friendship afloat. You can definitely count on her to be there. Just be sure you are as committed to the friendship as she is.

12-17 points: Choppy Waters

Sometimes it's hard to tell if your friend is casting you off or simply drowning with tons of other obligations. Like it or not, priorities change. A friend who may have had tons of hang time before can suddenly be out of radar contact when sports, after-school activities, and family time crowd her schedule. If it seems like she's making the effort when and where she can, it may be up to you to keep the friendship going. Be patient and supportive. She'll be grateful to you once her seas calm. And, hopefully, she'll remember how you stuck by her without demands and complaints.

18-24 points: Drowning Friendship

It sounds like your bud is a little too self-involved and thoughtless to know she's letting you down. If she has a few redeeming qualities, limit your friendship to a certain activity or time. If she's a fabulous set painter, by all means let her work on your scenery project and have a few laughs while you sketch…but that's about it. If you make a few attempts to keep the friendship afloat, but still feel that she's dumped you for new friends or a boy, it's time to pull up anchor and sail to better waters.

Friend Foes: What's a Girl to Do?

If your friendship is about to hit the rocks, you need to ask some tough questions and chart a smoother course.

How does each person feel?

This question could change your conclusion. You should always check to see how the other person in the relationship feels. Your best bet is to ask your friend what she thinks. If she wants out, maybe that's best for both sides. Then again, maybe it's you who wants to call it quits. You also need to recognize your own feelings about the friendship—and be honest with her.

Do you feel as if you're being used or ignored?

Those are not good things to feel. Pay attention to how your friend is treating you. Maybe it's best to get out of the relationship before you feel worse. Talk to your friend about how you feel. You may end up solving the problem, but if you don't, you should also consider a few more things.

How will splitting up affect you?

Will it be awkward sitting next to her in science class, or being in the same homeroom? Will she be on the same soccer team? It may be hard to maintain your cool if you have a lot of contact in your daily routines. Be extra nice to yourself during this tough time and remember that clear skies are ahead.

How will splitting up affect her?

This is a delicate matter and should be considered carefully. How well will your friend cope if you nix the

friendship? Think about it this way: What if you were on the receiving end? Would you want to be shrugged off, pushed away or just plain ignored? Consider how you would feel, and you'll see that you should still treat her with respect and kindness, even though you may not be friends anymore. So think about her, and decide. Should you stay or go? You probably know her well enough to determine how she will react and how much it will hurt her.

You decide to call it quits.

OK, so you've looked at your situation from all angles, and you've decided it's time to go your separate ways. The number one rule to breaking off a relationship: Don't be cruel. Sit own with your friend somewhere private, and explain that you think the two of you should part. It will probably be an emotional conversation, so be prepared. If you feel unsure of telling her in person, you may want to try it on the phone or write her a letter, but that's up to you and how you feel about her.

She decides to call it quits.

It's definitely difficult to listen to your friend tell you she no longer wants to be your bud. Remember that not everyone is brave enough to speak honestly and directly, so you should listen carefully and watch what's

HeLP!

My BFF and I have been friends for seven years, but I'm not sure I want to be friends with her anymore. We don't have anything in common, like I'm on the track team, and she's not. Should I ditch her or stick with it?

Just because you're not on the same team doesn't mean you have nothing in common! Most pairs don't share every single interest—how dull! If it's just track you don't share, what's the big deal? Aren't you guys into other stuff, like gabbing on the phone, Rollerblading, or going to the movies? You must share *some* things if you've been buds for seven years! However, if you find yourselves sitting in silence, breaking plans with each other and feeling bored, then it might be time to loosen the friendship reins. You don't have to dump her, but you also don't have to force a best friendship that isn't there. Acknowledge your differences, but stay on friendly terms. There's nothing like an old pal!

going on. Your first reaction might be anger or defensiveness. Retract your raw emotions, and instead of lashing out, handle the situation maturely. You are still a great person. So take a deep breath and respect her decision. If she's done being your friend, say, "Take care. I'll see you around school." Then…

Go out and try new things, like joining a sports team where you'll meet new friends. Feel good about yourself. As time passes, you'll realize that maybe this breakup worked out for the best. Take a step back. Look at your friend. Is she the same person you had become friends with in the first place? Probably not. Chances are, you'll meet new and better friends that you might not have met if you hadn't split.

YOUR HELP!

My BFF is such a huge flirt. She gets loud and giggly around boys! She's making a fool of herself.

Write your friend a note and explain how you feel. If she avoids you, try talking to her in person. Tell her to stop acting so flirty. Since you're friends, she will hopefully listen to you and understand your thoughts.
—Libby, 11

Tell your BFF that she should try to be her wonderful self around boys— smart, funny, etc. If this doesn't work, then try to avoid her in those situations.
—Carly, 12

I think you should tell your BFF to settle down. Explain that you think she's acting weird around boys. When you talk with her, make sure you are nice and that you don't yell or anything.
—Katie, 12

You should point out what your BFF is doing. Possibly, she's not aware of some of her actions. Explain that there are other ways of getting a boy's attention, such as talking to him.
—Nicole, 12

Ask her why she chooses to attract so much attention. Tell her people probably won't think very much of her if she continues to behave this way. Explain that boys will like her more if she isn't so loud.
—Courtney, 11

Friend Fights

Chapter 7

Bickering Buds

It doesn't matter how true-blue those bud-bonds are, sometimes the two of you are bound to argue.

You raid her closet, pore over her notes and borrow her coolest CDs. If you spent any more hang time with your best bud, you two would qualify for a clone study. As hard as it can be to imagine, there will probably come a day when things suddenly go wrong. *Way* wrong.

Friend fights hurt something awful. It may help to know that most friends eventually make up. And even though some friendships may fade, the really important ones actually get stronger after a few fights. When you argue with your friend, you're learning about each other's limits, values, and personalities. And although crawling beneath the bed covers to hide from a friend might seem easier than facing the fight head on, it's important to learn how to resolve a disagreement—and get your friendship nice and cozy again.

Take a Deep Breath

All those times you saw other buds battling, you thanked your stars it wasn't you and your bestest. Now it is. Harsh words were said, and you feel like the mac 'n' cheese you had for lunch is doing the Macarena. You can't even think about how you'll face the walk home from school...alone. As hard as this sounds, the first thing to do is to calm down. Heartbroken, upset, crying, steaming, fuming girls don't solve problems. You wouldn't work on a book report in this state, so you shouldn't work on something as important as a friendship! Give yourself time for those intense feelings to soften—they will eventually. Take a walk, listen to music, write in a journal, or even cry. You need time to think things through.

Figure Out Why You're Fighting

Now comes the hard part—trying to figure out what the fight is really all about. Sometimes what causes friends to get mad is entirely separate from what is hurting us. Take Jen and Sarah, both 12. Jen was furious when Sarah brought her a chocolate sundae when Jen asked for caramel: "She knows I like caramel!" Even as she got angry, Jen knew it was a silly

reason for a fight. It didn't take her long to realize what was really bothering her: "I had this awful feeling we were drifting apart. And then, after all our ice cream feasts, she couldn't keep my favorite flavor straight! It was like she was proving me right." Once Jen figured out what was really eating her, it was easier for her to get to the bottom of the problem.

While each fight is as unique as the pair of friends who have it, there are some common problems that fuel feuds. Read on to find more.

1 New Friend Freakouts

This problem is probably the most common—and the most painful. Just ask Jani, 13. She recently freaked when she and two friends had Friday night plans. They were going to bond

at the movies, then grab a snack. But the threesome agreed that if one friend had to bail, they would go Saturday instead. Well, Jani's mom said she had to baby-sit her little sister. So...Jani's two friends went ahead to the movie and out for a snack without her.

Jani was ticked. "I felt completely left out." She was especially peeved because she could've gone if her pals had rescheduled. But Jani got a funny feeling her buds wanted time without her. "It's like they didn't want me to go!"

Jani could have gone ballistic because her friends didn't keep their original plans to skip the flick fest. But that's not what was really making her angry. "I was jealous of them having fun while I spent the night pouring lemonade," says Jani. "But mostly I felt that they were ditching me."

What she did: Jani decided blowing up at her friends would do no good and maybe even make them more likely to leave her out the next time. She didn't really want an all-out apology—she just wanted to be sure they weren't purposely leaving her out. When Jani asked them, they told her they were just dying to get out of their houses—no ulterior motives. Jani felt reassured and things got back to normal. But what if they had been purposely blowing her off? Then it would have been time for Jani to get better buds that respect her.

Our advice: Give your friends the benefit of the doubt before you freak out. True friends are supportive, especially when they know that you were hurt by their action. If you accuse them of dumping you, they're only going to react as angrily as you did—and that doesn't help a friendship. If you remain calm and they're not supportive, don't sweat it (though it's hard not to). You surely have other, far more faithful, friends.

2 Hurtful Friends

Cara, 10, knows firsthand how hard it is when a friend is mean. Her friends were acting funny (like not waiting for her after school). Even before she heard the scoop—that they said she was a dork—Cara was completely crushed.

Her first instinct was to yell at them for what she heard they'd said. But after talking to her mom, she decided she would leave it alone.

What she did: "I wanted them to think I didn't care about what they said," Cara explains. "I was hurt, but I didn't want them to have the satisfaction of knowing." Cara knew she couldn't deal with such a mean bunch, so she made friends with new girls instead.

Our advice: Cara handled her cold-hearted friends well—though she didn't chew them out. It's perfectly fine to calmly confront friends when you're hurt, but it's also OK to ignore them completely. Some people don't deserve the attention you'd give them if you got really worked up. Cara, instead, did a good thing for herself. She put all the energy she would've used getting mad into making nicer friends.

❸ Talkin' About Each Other

Jessica, 11, recently had to cope when her friends told practically everybody but the principal that she was a snob. Jessica almost screamed her head off at them in band practice. She felt like hurling her flute across the room. (Thankfully, she didn't.)

What she did: "A couple of days later, I asked them why they said that," she says. After lots of listening, Jessica dragged it out of her pals. They were jealous of Jess's new buds from the basketball team. As much as the argument was a pain, everything turned out great. "We finally made up and everything's fine."

Our advice: Talking, listening, and being patient with pals is the best medicine to kill nasty remarks. You might have to dig to get to the bottom of their words, but if you find they have a beef with your behavior (like they did with Jessica's), be willing to compromise. Jessica made more of an effort to balance time with her new basketball friends with time with her old buds.

❹ Copy Cat

Have a friend who hits school with a new hot pink backpack the day after you got yours? Erin, 10, understands the frustration: "My copy cat best friend Sam always gets the same clothes I have. Then we show up wearing exactly the same thing, and people call us Twinkies." The boiling point came for Erin when she recently picked out some cool new sneaks. Sam liked them, too. So bam! Sam started sportin' the same trendy tennies. And Erin got mad.

What she did: After thinking it over and talking to her mom, Erin decided to be flattered that Sam liked her style enough to steal it. So Erin decided to be supportive. Erin talked to Sam and calmly explained that she (Sam) needed to explore her own style territory and that she (Erin) would gladly help her.

Our advice: The minute you try to say something to your copying bud, she may get defensive, so be super supportive and caring. Offering to help her select her own style is a good way to go. You might even get to the point where you can ask if she could help you sometimes, too! That way—oddly enough—she might be less inclined to copy you.

5 Boy Battles

This one's a big source of friendship strife. Katie, 11, is still steamed at her friend who was a tad too attentive to her crush. "I couldn't believe she'd do that! She knew how hurt I'd be."

What she did: Katie and her friend had a heart-to-heart. "I just told her she hurt me." The two girls aren't totally back together, nor is their relationship back to normal. But Katie hopes it will be soon.

Our advice: This is tricky territory for all friends. While you might think meeting your friend's crush for pizza is perfectly fine, your friend may not agree. You'll want to make it clear to

everyone that he's not your crush, just your friend. Tell your friend in advance about your plans and let her know that you aren't trying to push her jealousy buttons.

The bottom line is this: There's only one really good way to prevent boy battles—and that's to avoid them. It's never a good idea to get mixed up with the apple of your friend's eye—if you want to maintain your friendship.

6 Totally Stupid Stuff

Stupid fights are important, too—they usually let you know that you and your friend need a break. So if you two start seriously arguing over something silly, or, if you can't even remember what you're arguing about, it's time to call it quits for a day or two.

Remember, a little absence can make you and your friend even fonder of each other.

now what? make up!

"You can't stay mad forever," Katie, 12, says. Luckily, most friends get fed up with fighting. Time to put down your dukes and get familiar with these no-fail friend-fight fixer-uppers.

Arguments, hurt feelings, silent treatments, and harsh words are exactly what friend fights are made of—and that stinks! But the thing about a fight is, when it's over, your whole world feels happy and peaceful. Lots of times, the friendship gets stronger because the fight clears up underlying sore points that might have fueled the fight in the first place. When you're done reading these tried and true fight fixers, you'll know how to get back to that friendly feel-good place.

She's Mad At You...

1 Say you're sorry. When a friend lets you know she's upset about something you've said or done (or she thought you said or did), it's up to you to clear the air. Even if it's a misunderstanding—wait, especially if it's a misunderstanding—you should step up to the apology plate. Admitting you're sorry isn't easy, but if you do a hat dance around her now-sensitive feelings, the drama will just grow. To deliver a sincere apology,

Dear Maria,
I'm so sorry...

look your friend in the eye and say, "I'm sorry." Now hug, cry, do what you do, then go do something fun together. You've had enough serious discussion for one afternoon.

2 Write the wrong. You want her forgiveness but find it easier to write than to call or say so in person? Put it on pretty stationery and mail it with stickers and a cool stamp, or e-mail. She just might call the minute she reads it.

3 Picture her forgiveness. Sometimes, a thousand words aren't worth very much. Or maybe you're not a word person, which means saying or writing an apology would be like hiking up Banana Peel Mountain in six-inch platforms. Non-word people are usually either visual-artsy or have a thing for math. And since calculating a serious algebra equation isn't all that heart-warming, this fight-fixer is for the art lovin' gal. Draw, paint, sketch a picture that screams, "You're awesome, and I'm sorry for not seeing the hurtfulness of what I did!" Mount the picture on a piece of poster board and, at the top center, expertly write her name in oversized block letters. Deliver it to her with a smile. If your masterpiece doesn't muster peace, it's back to the drawing board, Lady Picasso. Read on.

4 Make her a gift. How about a framed picture of the two of you

Should your friendship be saved?

Most friendships are worth fixing. But there are times, when the question isn't how do you get back on track, but should you? You have to decide if the friendship is really worth the heartache you're going through to save it.

But before you decide, ask yourself:

1. What exactly were the circumstances?
Make sure you're clear on what happened. Did she know she was supposed to meet you at the time you mentioned? Be sure you find out how things look from her side.

2. Did my friend deliberately hurt me?
This is a biggie. Nobody needs unkind friends who are out to destroy them. But sometimes friends don't realize that they've caused you hurt. Sometimes friends learn what you find acceptable and unacceptable from times when you've gotten upset.

3. Can I trust my friend again?
Maybe she isn't the school's greatest secret keeper. You just have to be able to feel as though you can safely give her your whole-hearted friendship again—without getting yourself majorly hurt. If the answer is you can't but you still like her, maybe you can make the friendship more casual.

4. Do my friend and I fight more than we have fun?
Having fun together is what friendships are all about. If you spend most of the time at odds, chances are your friendship has run its course.

during better times? Or, a candle you made just for her at one of those fun craft-making stores? All other gift ideas are subject to details only you know about your friend. The more personal, the better. Wrap your package in homemade wrapping paper (sponge-paint some plain white paper), and present it to her in private.

5 **Give in.** That's right. Swallow your pride, and let it slide—even though you "absotively, posilutely" know for sure that you did so pay her back the five dollars you borrowed from her. She's peeved, and you're left wondering if she's having a brain lapse or something. So why should you say "sorry"? Well, let's put this in perspective. Is it really worth losing a friend over a five-spot? Offer up a hard-to-resist compromise: "I'll tell you what, let's scarf down five dollars worth of Baskin Robbins, my treat, and call it even." If she insists on having it her way, cough up the $5 and consider it an investment in the friendship. Even if she is having a brain lapse, she's your bud and was nice enough to float you the moolah to begin with. Oh, and next time you pay her back on a loan, ask for a receipt. Nicely.

You're Mad At Her...

6 **Let your fingers do the walking.** All right, you're upset.

Maybe you're fuming. That's fine. Let yourself be mad. But be mad in a pair of running shoes while you jog a mile. Be mad at your pillow while you pulverize those teeny goose feathers. Just don't unleash your inner Cruella on your friend because that can create mutual madness, which would really blow things out of proportion. The heat of your feelings will cool down and, when you're done seeing red, simply call Miss Knucklehead and tell her what's up: "Did you know you really bummed me out the other day when you blurted my business in front of everyone? Can you promise not to do it again?" If so, great. That'd be enough said.

7 **Forever hold your peace.** If it's a little more complicated than that, and forgiving her becomes a chore on your to-do list, first decide if a Fixer is really the best option. Question: Was this a premeditated Ice Queen move, or was she totally unaware she'd driven a stake through your heart? Was this the first time your friend did whatever she did to make you mad, or does she do this to you all the time? For a repeat offender, see Fight Fixer No. 10. If your friend's offense was a first-time flub, why not chalk it up to a she's-only-human mistake and forget about it? Turning the other cheek on her out-of-character moment is very mature of you and will help you "walk away" mentally,

which miraculously squashes the drama you're feeling emotionally. In other words, don't say—or do— a darn thing.

8 Ask and ye shall receive. Depending on what's happened, a formal apology may be the only way your friend can atone for her sins. If you need a sincere "I'm sorry" to get over her infraction, that's OK. But you might have to ask for it. She can't read your mind, and chances are she feels bad about the fight, too. Hey, maybe she's reading Fight Fixers 1 through 5 right now, trying to map out her apology strategy. Make it easy for her. Send an e-mail explaining that if she were to apologize and make a promise it won't happen again, that'd be enough for you.

9 Pick a punishment. The word "punish" might bring to mind images

of six consecutive weekends grounded with no TV, IM, or sleepovers because you accidentally borrowed your dad's drill to crack walnuts on the antique dining room table. Banish that thought! Seriously, though, pick a dare for your bud to prove she's sorry. Put ketchup, mustard, and horseradish on a pickle and tell her to eat it. Ask her to wear that hot pink sweatshirt saying "My grandma loves me" that her granny got her as a gift last year—to school. Have her carry your lunch tray for a week. Think of something just painful enough to be funny, but not hurtful. When she's done, pinkie swear to be more careful with each other's feelings.

10 Sign a contract. Say you tried a Fight Fixer but, despite your best efforts, you're still not over it. We'll call this "fight residue," which is just mistrust wearing an everything's-OK-now mask. There's a China-sized crack of doubt that she might let you down again, or maybe she's a tiny bit worried you're not totally healed from being hurt. Luckily, you can swat away these emotional mosquitoes with a contract. On a piece of light-colored paper, write a list of ways you promise to be good to each other. Then, carefully tear the perimeter so all sides are rough-edged. Scrunch the paper into a ball, unscrunch it, and dip it in room-temperature tea until it looks aged. Gently lay it out flat in the sun and, when it's dry, you'll have an official, homemade Bill of Friendship Rights. Suggestion: Make two so you don't fight over who gets to keep it!

Mutual Madness...

11 Break the ice. Silence is a super common side effect of a fight. You both think it's up to the other person to admit she's obviously lost her mind. So why should you be the one to initiate a truce? You can keep feeling angry and hurt, or you can decide you'd rather have fun and feel happy. Gee, let's see, which shall it be! E-mail her, call, write a note—just make it clear that doing nothing will get your friendship nowhere. Do what you have to in order to get this ball rolling. If she doesn't respond, see below.

12 Wait for her. What do you do if you're so completely over this rift between you two...yet, she still won't cave? It's tempting to want to bail from the friendship and let her wallow in her stubborn anger. But that's the easy way out. If you think you've done your share in trying to mend the situation, you're probably right. But you can't force her into anything. So, you'll wait. Try not to hold it against her if she needs more time than you do to cool off. She'll come around.

13 Contest the outcome. Who's going to win this big hairy attitude brawl!? You are! She is! Oh, wait. Tell yourselves it's time to deal. Ask her to come to your house in cruddy old clothes Saturday afternoon. Pre-date, bust open your piggy bank and buy two dozen eggs and two candy bars. When she arrives, give her a dozen eggs, keep a dozen for yourself, and have an egg toss in the backyard. Throw an egg right at her T-shirt or jeans. If she looks at you like you've cracked, "egg" her on to throw hers at you by breaking one on your head. If you're both not covered in egg and laughing within a few minutes, you blew this assignment. The candy bars are for you guys to eat afterward as you glow in renewed friendship...and yolk.

14 Exorcise with exercise. This is about working it out by working out. You're both going to sweat it out, side by side, until you decide together when enough is enough. A little healthy competition will replace the spat you're having over who did what and who's right and all that other poppycock. Race around the school track, do pull-ups, push-ups, or sit-ups—counting aloud, until one of you drops. When you're sweaty, fatigued, ready for a time out, say, "I'm sick of it all, especially being in a fight with you." Ten bucks says she'll share her sports drink in agreement.

Beware—Tricky Friendships ahead!

FriendShip FreakoutS!

Wouldn't be great if your friend's interests, habits and actions were always 100% in sync with yours? You guys could all get crushes at the same time, be into all the same bands, and enjoy all the same cool activities. Well, here's a shocker. Life just doesn't work that way!

That's why, at some point along the line, you might find yourself at a cross-road with your friends. Maybe you'll feel like you've outgrown them a little—and would love a chance to hang with an older crew. Or maybe—yikes, they might suddenly get into stuff you have no desire to get into—like not good-for-you stuff? Read on.

Older Friends

You've been part of the same group since you were seven, and you totally dig it. This year, though, you can't help feeling you're a little more, well, mature than some of the girls in your group. When it comes to fashion, boys, or music, you're on a whole different level. Your gals are still loving Britney, for example, while you're so into Shakira.

That's why you were psyched when Vanessa, who's 14, invited you to sit with her crew on the bus. You two really hit it off and you've been hanging out ever since. Vanessa's totally cool. She showed you how to put on make-up and do a French manicure. She even has a totally cute BF! She's so smart and confident that you take every word of her advice as total gospel. So what if she's older? True friendship has nothing to do with digits, right?

Well, that depends. Older friends can indeed come with some pretty awesome benefits, especially if they have viewpoints and interests you can get behind. Weirdness can arise, though, if your older bud is into stuff you're just not about. Digging the same music is a start, but the friendship likely won't go the distance unless you have more in common. Here are some older bud ups and downs to help you figure out the age bracket racket.

An Older Friend Rocks When...

❧ *She has a totally positive vibe.* Hanging with an older bud who feels great about herself and says "See ya" to stuff that's no good for her can be really inspirational and empowering. It's cool to follow her lead and, trust the life experience she has under her belt. Lauren totally admires her older BFF for making it through peer pressure and other tough stuff without dipping into any negatives: "She'll be my friend forever!"

❧ *She refuses to be a clone.* Every single girl in your group is probably sporting the same pair of blue flip-flops—as if they are the only cool slides in the world! Your new BFF is two years older than you and is so not into following the pack. She proudly flaunts her toesies in a fab-and-funky pair of silver platform sandals. She isn't afraid to be herself—and you're

loving her attitude because you've always been an individual, too. Such a great sense of confidence often grows stronger as you get older.

An Older Friend Is a Bummer When...

❧ *She peer pressures you.* If you don't approve of your older pal's social activities and if you feel she's leaning hard on you to join in, big trouble is brewing. You've heard it before, and it's true: You should never cave in to peer pressure or do anything that isn't good for you. Really, it's a matter of respect—the respect your buds should have for you and the respect you should have for yourself.

A true friend wants what's best for you. She knows your boundaries, and she doesn't step over them— that's respect. Flip the situation around. Would you want your friend to do something that would make her feel awful? Of course not. If your pal insists that you partake in whatever negative activity she is up to, blows up at you, or quits calling you, you haven't lost much. In fact, this person is saving you a ton of trouble, so wish her well and move on.

❖ *She makes you feel like a baby.*
An older bud is a bummer when she holds her age or experience over you! This is a total sign of immaturity. She's puffing her ego up because she feels small and insecure. Don't buy into such sorry hype. Let her know you want her to see you as an equal, not her "younger" friend. A sincere friend will treat you with respect all the time, no matter your age difference.

❖ *She ignores you.*
Say your new, older friend is super-nice when you two are alone, hanging out at the youth center or whatever. But when you see her in school on Monday, she acts like you're invisible.

So what's ignoring someone really about? Looking like she's powerful. Ridiculous, right? Totally. But some girls actually think they seem really important and in control when they act like another human being isn't even worth acknowledging. True-blue buds don't belittle each other this way. Your smart solution: Find a cooler friend!

The Test 'o Time.
Hanging with older friends can work if you stay true to who you are. Don't bend like a twisty straw just to have a few so-called cool friends accept you. No matter what age your buds are, the key is to make sure the friends you're rollin' with make your life better, not worse.

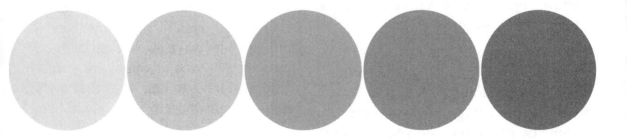

Hey! not me!

Sure, you knew some girls your age would start to experiment with stuff—but you hadn't figured it would be your friends.

In that cool picture from last summer of you and your buds, you're all standing in a row, arms linked with matching smiles and tankinis. Whether that picture actually lives on your dresser or only in your mind, you remember the happy feeling of being part of the group.

But things have changed since then. Your friends are exploring new paths, some of which make you not-so-comfy. Maybe your whole group hasn't gone astray, but just your BFF. You've known her for a trillion years, but suddenly she's transformed into this, well, not exactly terrific person. You want to remain friends, but you wish she'd stop acting so high-and-mighty, weird, flirty, whatever.

As much as you'd like the power to turn your BFF magically back to the pal she used to be, you're not Sabrina. So what to do? Here are some pointers to guide you through.

1 Why have things gotten complicated? It was so simple when your biggest debate with buds was whether to play Pictionary or Monopoly. Sometimes you got your way; sometimes you didn't. But now, with friends venturing into iffy or off-limits territory, you feel pulled in different directions.

Whether your friends are sneaking around the rules, bending them a bit, or boldly smashing them to smithereens, part of you probably wants to hang on to them. You might even think they're um, a tad cool because they're daring or being rebellious. A little thrill's not such a bad thing, right? But what if what they're doing isn't so healthy, like smoking? If you're associated with something a wee bit shady for your taste, you have to deal with that awful, anxious sensation in your chest, like a hand squeezing your heart.

Things also get complicated if what your buds want and what you want don't always jive. If this stuff feels tough, it's because this stuff *is* tough. Give yourself a pat on the back for realizing you have a dilemma. It's the first step in figuring out some real solutions!

2 What's wrong with me? Of course, being part of a tight group feels terrific. If you're having a yucky day, relating to your buds can give your self-confidence a reassuring boost. But the opposite is also true. If you're not doing what your friends are doing, you might worry something is wrong with you.

Girls who lead their packs often seem older and more confident to many of their pack-members. It's easy to think of these girls as having fun 24/7—and being way more popular than you and others who aren't in the fast lane. But, chances are these leaders of the pack of fun don't necessarily feel as cool and confident on the inside as they look from the outside.

But since they always look so cool and confident, then YOU start second-guessing yourself. Are you hopelessly uncool? Terminally infantile? Although some girls are tempted to do "bad" things to prove they're OK or to impress their buds, this strategy is usually a dud. Ever see a girl trying too hard to wear makeup? She doesn't look glamorous—she looks clownish.

Finally, remember that social, emotional, and physical changes come at different times for different girls. There's never a perfect timetable. Even if all your friends are way ahead of you, relax. Growing up is not a race, and no one is watching the clock. Bottom line: If you don't feel right doing something, it's probably wrong. Waiting until you are ready to do stuff—or deciding it'll never be right for you—is always a good thing.

3 Am I going to lose all my friends? Some girls dread being separated from their friends, even for a minute. So the thought of being worlds apart emotionally or socially is scary. You may worry that if you don't go along with the group, your buds will kick you out of the clique.

As Mira, 11, puts it, "I'm always the one saying, 'Maybe we shouldn't,' like I'm the mother or something. Maybe they think I'm no fun anymore?" Henny, 11, says, "Sometimes my friends are like, 'Come on, just try it.' If I say I don't want to, they might not want me around." Although we can't give you airtight guarantees, it's unlikely that your truest-bluest buds will toss you off just because you say, "No thanks," to something. You wouldn't have chosen such superficial clods in the first place as friends, right?

It's possible, though, that some of your friends might choose to hang out with other girls. While this may be painful for you, remember that it's perfectly normal for friendships to change as you get older. Circles of friends always shift as you meet new people and find you have more in common with some than with others. This doesn't mean there's anything wrong with you—it's just that you're taking different paths.

4 Should I cover for my friend? Aaargh! You need King Solomon, or someone at least as wise, to figure out what to do when a friend begs you to help—but the favor makes you break out in hives. Erin, 10, says "My best friend was out of school for a while and had to make up a big science test, so she asked to see mine." Since Erin's teacher had asked everyone not to do exactly that, she was in a terrible jam.

YOUR HELP!

My BFF is totally obsessed with her weight. She always asks me if I think she is fat. She's not fat, and she's driving me crazy. What should I do?

Help your friend love her body. Encourage her to be healthy, and re-assure her that she is NOT fat. Tell her it makes you sad when she puts herself down.

—Jackie, 12

Have a private talk with your BFF. Tell her she's not fat and that her complaining gets on your nerves. If she keeps it up, ignore her or remind her again she's not fat. And that even if she were, you guys would still be best buds.

—Clare, 13

I would sit down with my BFF and have a talk with her. I'd tell her she isn't fat. If she still thinks she's fat, then I would get help from a school counselor.

—Ashley, 12

"I felt terrible," Erin says, "because she's my good friend and really needed help. Friends should help." Like Erin, however, you may feel torn when doing right by your friend puts you in the wrong. Erin realized, "Giving her the test would be the same as cheating." She also worried that helping her bud was too risky: "I knew my teacher would figure out that someone showed her a test, and I could get in big trouble with the honors committee."

It's important to remember that being a good friend doesn't mean you have to violate your own values or honor code. You can choose a different path from your friend without totally abandoning her. In fact, if she's a really good bud, she will care about your feelings too. She wouldn't want you to do something that makes you feel low or that could get you in trouble.

You can tell your friend you want to help her but have to find a different way. Try saying, "Let's see if we can think of what else will help you." In Erin's case, offering to tutor her friend was a workable solution. That way, she helped her friend without compromising her own honesty.

5 Will people think I'm bad news, too? You've probably heard a parent or other adult say, "You're judged by the company you keep." You may have found this to be somewhat true if, say, you sit at the loudest table in the lunchroom—the one that's always giving the cafeteria monitor a hard time.

Even if you're the quietest girl in your group, never talk back, and always bus your tray, the cafeteria monitor judges you as a group. This is called "guilt by association." Same goes for when you're hanging with buds who get caught doing something bad. Despite your innocence, sometimes you go down, too. That's a risk you take.

But it's also true that you can definitely remain your own person, even when your best bud is way different. In fact, sometimes opposites attract. We often find pals who are abundant in the traits we think are lacking in ourselves!

6 Should I stop being friends with her? When your friend does the very thing your parents have drilled into your head *not* to do, you may think, "That's it. She's history. If my folks find out what she's up to, they'll put an instant kabosh on the friendship." You yourself may think this drastic solution is the only one.

Not necessarily. Rather than ditching your friend, pick and choose when and how you'll see her. Maybe you'll decide just hanging in school is best. Or that it's OK to invite her to your house, but not go to hers. Or you may feel comfortable being with her when adults are handy, but not at unsupervised places. Another possibility is that you'll avoid one-on-one situations, but you'll include this friend when others are around.

If none of these solutions quite work and you definitely want to cool the friendship, you can avoid an ugly mess by doing it gradually. You don't have to stage a scene. That way, you're also keeping the door open to the possibility of getting together again, if in the future you feel more comfortable hanging with her.

7 What if I'm worried about my friend? Let's say your friend is doing stuff that's totally not OK—not just in bad taste, but dangerous. Beyond deciding to avoid the activity yourself, what should you do?

If you find yourself wondering whether your friend's behavior is normal or scary, it's a good idea to ask an adult for advice. You can't expect to know all the answers. So talk to a parent, school guidance counselor, or trusted teacher. If you're concerned about your friend's privacy, don't give her name. The important thing is that you and an adult figure out a way to get your friend help if she needs it. She may not appreciate it at first, but that's being a good friend.